How To Grow
Annuals

By the Editors of Sunset Books
and Sunset Magazine

Lane Books • Menlo Park, California

Acknowledgments

We are extremely grateful to the many people who generously contributed their knowledge, skills, advice, and time to this book. Special thanks go to Eileen Larsen for her assistance with research and text; to Richard Dunmire *(Sunset Magazine)*, the Ferry-Morse Seed Company and Elmer Twedt (plant breeder and botanist) for their invaluable advice and consultation; and to photographer Ells Marugg who traveled many miles and visited many gardens with our editors.

Edited by Richard Osborne

Design: John Flack, JoAnn Masaoka
Illustrations: Gary J. Patterson

On the cover: State Fair zinnias against a background of 'White Cascade' petunias. Photographer: Ells Marugg.

Executive Editor, Sunset Books: David E. Clark

Contents

Annuals: Quick-Color Superstars

Famous for their flowers, annuals will brighten any garden, lend gay splashes of color to patios and terraces, and be a constant reminder of the outdoors when brought into your house as cut flowers.

Not only do you get a summerlong abundance of flowers from annuals but also you get it quickly. Speed merchants of the gardening world, they provide maximum bloom in minimum time. Plant annual seeds in the spring and you'll be rejoicing in bloom by summer. Or if you want immediate satisfaction, small annual plants sold in nurseries will flower within just a few weeks of planting. Annuals truly are quick-color superstars.

Certainly gay and pretty, annuals are also versatile. Want flowers in a sunny spot of the garden? Try zinnias. A splash of color in the shade? Cineraria will give it to you. Problems with a damp area? Give *Mimulus tigrinus* a chance. Want to cut down on watering? Rely on verbena. Whether you want just a few flowers to brighten the porch, a plant to cheer up a difficult garden corner, or a dozen different flowers to landscape the entire yard, you'll find an annual that is suitable.

What is an annual?

Though perhaps best known simply as flowers, annuals are described by botanists as plants whose life cycle is completed in a single growing season: the seed germinates; the plant grows, blooms, sets seed, and then dies. In their single-season life span, annuals are distinct from perennial and biennial plants. Perennials live on from year to year, flowering and setting seed during the warm months, becoming dormant during the cold season, and returning to activity again when the weather warms up. Biennials, like annuals, die after setting seed, but rather than flower and produce seed in a single growing season, they require two seasons, growing into mature plants the first year, flowering and setting seed in their second year.

There are many, many kinds of annuals. Some, such as dill and corn, you probably know as a food seasoning or a vegetable. Others, you probably have pulled up as weeds.

The annuals in this book, and the annuals you'll want to grow, are those which are prized for their flowers and/or foliage. They include asters, bachelor's buttons, celosia, fairy primrose, marigolds, nasturtiums, pansies, petunias, sweet peas, and zinnias—to name but a few.

Within the group of annual flowers, there is certainly something for everyone. With a little planning and timed planting, you can enjoy successive bursts of color from earliest spring to the end of autumn (and even through the winter, if you live in a mild climate). You'll find annuals to brighten the entire garden or just a corner of it. Perhaps you want a colorful seasonal ground cover for fading spring bulbs or a vine to screen the patio during summer: try forget-me-nots, baby blue eyes, or morning glory vine. Annuals are excellent for filling in while young shrubs are maturing. And most make perfect container plants. Whatever your pleasure, you'll find that annuals are easy on the pocket book and return your investment many times over in satisfaction.

Annual flowers are among the plants that commercial seedsmen and plant breeders constantly experiment with to produce new varieties and types with new colors. The general trend in this breeding is towards shorter, sturdier plants with longer lasting, larger, and more profuse flowers, ones that are more disease-resistant than past annuals.

Each year you are likely to find seeds for new varieties of your favorite annuals. When shopping for seeds, you might like to try them. The flowers, both new and old, that are often considered the most outstanding are those with "All-America" printed on the seed packet. These plants have been proven in test gardens sponsored by various professional nursery and plant breeding organizations, and you'll be assured of getting viable seeds and strong, healthy plants.

In the encyclopedia section (pages 24–63) are descriptions of all the most popular annual flowers and some attractive lesser-known types. Information on each annual includes planting times, cultural requirements, and plant and flower descriptions. Look for the color photograph of each flower and suggestions for using and combining it in the garden or in containers.

Among the recommended varieties in the encyclopedia are some called *dwarf.* These are compact plants, usually growing shorter and bushier than the regular varieties. They are especially suitable for edgings, containers, and small borders.

Not all the plants listed in the encyclopedia are annuals; some are biennials whose leisurely growth has been speeded up by seedsmen and plant breeders so that they function as annuals; others are tender perennials—plants that live through the winter only in the most ideal circumstances and function as annuals in harsh climates.

How seeds grow

Have you ever watched a seed germinate—go through that wonderful transformation from an apparently insignificant bit of matter into a living plant? The drawings below show the process. If you'd like to see it for yourself, place about 6 nasturtium seeds between pieces of moistened paper towel on a dish in a warm, dark closet. Keep the towels damp, and in a week or two the beginnings of life should appear.

If a seed is viable, it will germinate (sprout). Most annual flower seeds you're likely to grow will take between one and three weeks to germinate—*exactly* how long depends on the type of seed and a fine balance of both external and internal factors. Moisture, warmth, and oxygen must be available in just the right amounts; then many changes take place simultaneously within the seed. First, the seed absorbs water and begins to swell as the seed coat softens. Next, enzyme activity increases, dissolving stored food and making it available to the growing embryo. Soon the seed coat splits and the first *hypocotyl* (primary root) appears. As the primary root grows downward, the *epicotyl* (stem) and foliage leaves emerge.

This describes what is known as hypogeous germination (see art below) in which the *cotyledons* (seed leaves) develop beneath the soil. In another form of germination, the seed leaves are pushed up from the ground and develop above the soil, withering and falling away as the true foliage leaves develop.

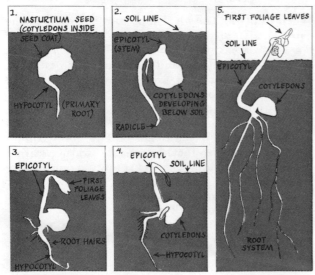

NASTURTIUM seed germination: seed leaves develop beneath soil (hypogeous germination); with some other seeds they develop above ground and are first to appear.

A close look at flowers

Flowers are certainly a main feature of annuals. Without them, most annuals would have no more appeal than weeds. Flowers come in a tremendously wide range of sizes, shapes, colors, and forms, but each plays a similar role in the life of the plant as the mechanism for reproduction. And as different as two flowers may appear, they usually have the same basic features necessary for producing seeds.

All but a few annual flowers take one of two basic forms. On flowers such as pansies, petunias, and poppies, flower petals surround one or more *stamens* (the male, pollen-bearing part) and the female *pistil* (which includes the ovaries). Pollen forms in the *anthers* at the tip of each stamen. When released, the pollen contacts the *stigma* at the tip of the pistil and works its way down through the tubelike *style* to the ovules at the bottom of the pistil which then develop into seeds.

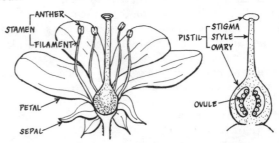

ON CONTACT with stigma, pollen from anthers travels down style to fertilize ovules, which develop into seeds.

The other common type of blossom appears on annuals in the Compositae family which includes such well-known plants as asters, marigolds, and zinnias. On these annuals, what is often mistakenly thought of as a single flower is actually a flower cluster composed of many flowers (and often two different kinds). Thus what you might think of as a petal is actually a whole flower.

Many flowers in this book are described as *double*. This indicates that there is more than one set of petals (or, in the case of composites, flowers) overlapping each other in the same blossom or head. Double flowers are generally fuller than single flowers.

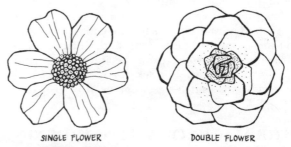

SINGLE flowers have only one set of petals (or one set of flowers if they are a composite such as cineraria); double flowers have several sets of petals or flowers.

Planting Tips and Garden Care

Whether you want a garden showcase of annuals or just a pot of flowers, your main concern will be the same: placing the plants in your garden or container and keeping them happily blooming.

You can get annuals either by growing them from seeds or buying them as small plants from a nursery. There are advantages and disadvantages to both; growing annuals from seed will give you more plants for your money, but seeds require a long time and a lot of work before they become flower-bearing plants. Nursery plants, on the other hand, are more expensive than seeds, but they don't require as much attention and time before turning your garden into something other than bare ground.

One of the most important factors in successful annual gardening is choosing plants that will be happy in the locations you want to plant them. If you don't select carefully, you'll have to provide necessary growing conditions artificially or be content with less than perfect results.

WHICH ANNUAL FOR YOU?

Deciding which annuals you are going to grow is the first step you'll take before actually planting. If you don't already have in mind the annuals you'd like, think of what you want from annuals—color, fragrance, texture, flower shape, plant height—and consider where you want to plant—in sun, shade, partial shade, containers. With these factors in mind, thumb through the encyclopedia on pages 24–63, look at the photographs of each flower, and pick out the plants that sound most attractive to you, will grow well where you are going to plant them, and will best fill your garden needs. If you have a specific annual in mind, select a place in the garden for it that will provide the conditions that it needs for healthy growth.

THE MAGIC OF SEED GARDENING

Once you've decided which plants you're going to grow, you are ready to get them into the ground or a container. Perhaps the most exciting way of growing annuals is from seeds. All ages of gardeners enjoy watching a tiny seedling inch its way up from bare ground and slowly develop into a full-fledged plant.

Seeds are available from most nurseries, from mail order catalogues, and from seed racks at many hardware stores and supermarkets. Or you might like to try seed tapes, a commercial idea intended to save time and work (see page 14). You can plant seeds in the garden right where they are to grow or start them in flats and then transplant the seedlings into their permanent home.

Sowing seeds in the garden

The big advantage of sowing seeds directly in the garden (as opposed to sowing in flats) is that you won't need to transplant the seedlings later in the season. And since transplanting is a growth retarding shock, your plants will flower sooner. Many gardeners feel that they get not only the most plants for their money by sowing seeds in the garden but also plants that will grow more vigorously and have a longer blooming period.

When to plant. The ideal time to plant seeds in the garden is after all danger of frost has passed but before hot weather has set in for the summer. This allows the seeds to germinate and the seedlings to establish themselves before hot weather stimulates rapid growth—a strain on young plants.

If you plant too early, frost can kill the seedlings, or the cold, wet ground cause poor germination and retarded growth. If you plant too late, the seedlings may be burned by the hot sun, the warm weather can force the immature plants to grow too quickly—resulting in sparse, thin foliage and small flowers—or your plants may not have time to mature and flower before autumn frosts kill them off.

In frost-free climates, open-ground seeding generally can get under way in February. April or May, or after all danger of frost has passed, are good months to begin seeding in most other areas. There are exceptions: in areas with a very short growing season, seeds that take a long time to germinate can be planted in the fall, before frosts; in areas with a long, cool growing season, early to mid-summer may not be too late to start seeds of sturdy, fast-growing annuals.

The hard-frost chart (below) should offer a guide for planting times in your area. It tells when the last and first frosts generally occur. Seed packets also usually give the prime planting dates for different areas throughout the country.

Preparing the soil. If you or someone you know has gardened with only moderate success, one of the problems may have been inadequate soil preparation. Plants are like people: they need nutrients, air, and water to live. Plants get these essentials primarily through their roots from the soil. The better the soil provides them, the better the plants will grow.

Ideal soil is loose enough to allow water and air to penetrate to the plant's roots. It should hold enough water to provide for the plants, yet not retain it like a sponge, for this can waterlog and eventually rot the roots. The soil must also provide nutrients and be loose enough for the roots to spread out easily.

Often, soil may only need to be turned and loosened and the clods broken up to a depth of about 8 to 12 inches. If you're just planting a small area, use a shovel or spading fork to turn the soil; otherwise, you'll save yourself back aches and blisters by renting or borrowing a power rotary cultivator to turn the soil.

If, in turning the soil, you notice that it is especially heavy, thick, and clayish or sandy and loose, to avoid later disappointment you should take extra preparative measures.

If the soil is too hard and packed to turn to the depth of a shovel blade, soak it deeply with water, let it dry for a day or two (so you won't be working with mud) and then try turning it. Repeat the soaking, if necessary, until the soil can be cultivated easily.

Humus or other organic material—such as peat moss, ground bark, compost, leaf mold, or manure—will generally improve most soils by insuring aeration, providing nutrients, and allowing good drainage with adequate water retention.

AVERAGE HARD-FROST DATES*

Based on U.S.D.A. weather records

State	Last in Spring	First in Fall	State	Last in Spring	First in Fall	State	Last in Spring	First in Fall
Alabama, N.W.	Mar. 25	Oct. 30	Kansas	Apr. 20	Oct. 15	Ohio, No.	May 6	Oct. 15
Alabama, S.E.	Mar. 8	Nov. 15	Kentucky	Apr. 15	Oct. 20	Ohio, So.	Apr. 20	Oct. 20
Arizona, No.	Apr. 23	Oct. 19				Oklahoma	Apr. 2	Nov. 2
Arizona, So.	Mar. 1	Dec. 1	Louisiana, No.	Mar. 13	Nov. 10	Oregon, W.	Apr. 17	Oct. 25
Arkansas, No.	Apr. 7	Oct. 23	Louisiana, So.	Feb. 20	Nov. 20	Oregon, E.	June 4	Sept. 22
Arkansas, So.	Mar. 25	Nov. 3						
			Maine	May 25	Sept. 25	Pennsylvania, W.	Apr. 20	Oct. 10
California			Maryland	Apr. 19	Oct. 20	Pennsylvania, Cen.	May 1	Oct. 15
Imperial Valley	Jan. 25	Dec. 15	Massachusetts	Apr. 25	Oct. 25	Pennsylvania, E.	Apr. 17	Oct. 15
Interior Valley	Mar. 1	Nov. 15	Michigan, Upper Pen.	May 25	Sept. 15			
Southern Coast	Jan. 15	Dec. 15	Michigan, No.	May 17	Sept. 25	Rhode Island	Apr. 25	Oct. 25
Central Coast	Feb. 25	Dec. 1	Michigan, So.	May 10	Oct. 8			
Mountain Sections	Apr. 25	Sept. 1	Minnesota, No.	May 25	Sept. 15	S. Carolina, N. W.	Apr. 1	Nov. 8
Colorado, West	May 25	Sept. 18	Minnesota, So.	May 11	Oct. 1	S. Carolina, S. E.	Mar. 15	Nov. 15
Colorado, N. E.	May 11	Sept. 27	Mississippi, No.	Mar. 25	Oct. 30	S. Dakota	May 15	Sept. 25
Colorado, S. E.	May 1	Oct. 15	Mississippi, So.	Mar. 15	Nov. 15			
Connecticut	Apr. 25	Oct. 20	Missouri	Apr. 20	Oct. 20	Tennessee	Apr. 10	Oct. 25
			Montana	May 21	Sept. 22	Texas, N. W.	Mar. 21	Nov. 10
Delaware	Apr. 15	Oct. 25				Texas, N. E.	Apr. 15	Nov. 1
District of Columbia	Apr. 11	Oct. 23	Nebraska, W.	May 11	Oct. 4	Texas, So.	Feb. 10	Dec. 15
			Nebraska, E.	Apr. 15	Oct. 15			
Florida, No.	Feb. 25	Dec. 5	Nevada, W.	May 19	Sept. 22	Utah	Apr. 26	Oct. 19
Florida, Cen.	Feb. 11	Dec. 28	Nevada, E.	June 1	Sept. 14			
Florida, South of Lake Okeechobee, almost frost-free			New Hampshire	May 23	Sept. 25	Vermont	May 23	Sept. 25
			New Jersey	Apr. 20	Oct. 25	Virginia, No.	Apr. 15	Oct. 25
Georgia, No.	Apr. 1	Nov. 1	New Mexico, No.	Apr. 23	Oct. 17	Virginia, So.	Apr. 10	Oct. 30
Georgia, So.	Mar. 15	Nov. 15	New Mexico, So.	Apr. 1	Nov. 1			
Idaho	May 21	Sept. 22	New York, W.	May 10	Oct. 8	Washington, W.	Apr. 10	Nov. 15
Illinois, No.	May 1	Oct. 8	New York, E.	May 1	Oct. 15	Washington, E.	May 15	Oct. 1
Illinois, So.	Apr. 15	Oct. 20	New York, No.	May 15	Oct. 1	W. Virginia, W.	May 1	Oct. 15
Indiana, No.	May 1	Oct. 8	N. Carolina, W.	Apr. 15	Oct. 25	W. Virginia, E.	May 15	Oct. 1
Indiana, So.	Apr. 15	Oct. 20	N. Carolina, E.	Apr. 8	Nov. 1	Wisconsin, No.	May 17	Sept. 25
Iowa, No.	May 1	Oct. 2	N. Dakota, W.	May 21	Sept. 13	Wisconsin, So.	May 1	Oct. 10
Iowa, So.	Apr. 15	Oct. 9	N. Dakota, E.	May 16	Sept. 20	Wyoming, W.	June 20	Aug. 20
						Wyoming, E.	May 21	Sept. 20

*Allow 10 days either side of above dates to meet local conditions and seasonal differences.

Spread about 2 to 3 inches of the organic material over the planting area and thoroughly mix it into the soil with a shovel or rotary tiller to a depth of about 9 inches; also add 3 to 5 pounds of bone meal or super phosphate per 100 square feet of soil. To heavy, clayish soils add gypsum (if soil is alkaline) or lime (if soil is acid) which will cause soil particles to combine into larger crumbs, improving drainage and workability. (See your county agricultural agent to find out your soil type and the amount of lime or gypsum to use.)

All this preparation to plant just a few flowers may seem like more work than it is worth, but once the soil has been conditioned thoroughly, you can rest assured that your plants may do their very best. And in the following years your soil preparation tasks will be much easier—just turning the soil and adding fertilizer or organic material to replenish nutrients.

How to sow seeds. On the back of each seed packet you'll find instructions for sowing and often recommendations for sowing in rows or broadcasting to grow clumps of plants. In either sowing method, first smooth the prepared planting bed with a rake, breaking up any clods of earth, then dampen the soil with a fine spray of water.

If you are sowing in rows, make the furrows about ¼ inch deep with a hoe or trowel. Space the furrows the distance apart recommended on the seed packet. Carefully sprinkle the seeds in the rows or broadcast them over planting area; cover with about ¼ inch of

BEFORE PLANTING, turn soil with a shovel to loosen it and mix in organic matter.

SOW SEEDS in furrows made with trowel in planting bed for rows of plants. Scatter a few seeds per inch.

AFTER SOWING, cover seeds with about ¼" of soil and lightly mulch area with coarse sawdust, ground bark.

soil and lightly mulch the bed with coarse sawdust or ground bark. (Very small seeds can be mixed with sand to help you sow them evenly.) Firm the seeded bed with the back of a shovel or a hoe or a flat board to assure the seeds will make good contact with the soil.

Soak the bed with a fine mist spray. Be very careful not to disturb the seeds by watering with a strong jet of water. Go back and forth over the bed with the spray until the soil is well soaked. Let puddles of water soak in as they accumulate before continuing.

Rewater the bed whenever the soil under the mulch of sawdust or ground bark looks dry. It is very important not to let the seeds dry out while they are germinating.

When seeds sprout. A week or two after sowing, your seeds should begin to germinate (sprout). At this time it is important to take a few protective measures.

Birds, snails and slugs, and hot or windy days are your seedlings' enemies. Cover the seedlings with a wire or plastic mesh supported on a wooden frame or stakes to protect them from birds. On very hot days, protect the seedlings from wilting or being burned by careful watering and shading them with lath (see page 13) or a piece of cardboard bent into a tepee shape.

Spread a good commercial slug and snail bait around planted beds. Bait comes in both pellet and meal form. Pellet-type bait is easier to spread than meal bait, and, when dampened, some brands will dissolve into a meal form having the consistency of sawdust. On the other hand, pellets are often more attractive to curious children and pets while meal bait is not.

Be careful when using snail and slug bait: some brands are highly poisonous to pets and children, and pellets may look especially attractive to them. You might want to set the bait out only at night (the time snails and slugs feed) on dampened newspaper or tin foil and then remove it from the garden during the day. If you leave bait around the garden during the day, use either a meal or dissolving pellet type.

Weeding. Don't attempt to weed a bed until the seedlings have enough foliage for you to distinguish them from the weeds.

Thinning out. After two pairs of true leaves develop, thin crowded plants by removing them. (The thinned seedlings usually can be transplanted to another location if you are very careful.) If you live in a cool-summer area, follow the spacing instructions on the seed packet. In hot-summer climates, leave a little less space between plants so that their foliage will shade the soil and help keep the roots cool and moist.

Feeding. The idea in feeding annuals is to keep them growing fast. About 14 days after germination, feed the seedlings with liquid fertilizer that is high in nitrogen. Continue to feed lightly every 2 weeks until flower buds form, then use a food that is low in nitrogen and high in phosphorus and potassium. Sprinkle the plants with water after feeding to wash any fertilizer from the foliage; this will prevent the leaves from being burned by the chemicals in the fertilizer.

Watering. Overhead watering with a fine spray is satisfactory until buds start to open; after blossoms unfold, flood irrigate the soil beneath the plants whenever possible (or use a watering tube), since overhead watering may bend the plants or break off the blossoms. The best time to water is in the morning. Watering at night encourages fungus diseases while mid-afternoon sun can burn wet foliage. Water whenever the top inch of soil is dry. (Also see page 13.)

Sowing seeds in flats

Many gardeners find that it is easier to start seeds in flats or other containers rather than in the garden. In a flat, plants are isolated from the rest of the garden and the growing conditions can be more easily controlled. You can provide seedlings just the right kind of soil, move them around so they receive the proper degree of sun or shade, and because plants are confined to a small area, watering is easier, and disease and pests can be readily noticed and controlled. Sowing in flats is the best method for starting seeds that are expensive or very small, seeds that take a long time to germinate, and seeds that you want to start when the ground is still too cold and wet. By starting seeds in flats you can also avoid the long periods of bare soil in your garden that do very little for the landscape.

Nursery flats are convenient because they'll hold an entire packet of seeds and are low and easily stored. But you can use pots, boxes, or any other container, including coffee cans and cut-down milk cartons. The peat moss pots available in nurseries are especially convenient. Be sure to punch holes in the bottom of the container you use to allow for water drainage.

To take full advantage of sowing seeds in flats, you will need a protected place to keep the planted flats, especially if you sow during the winter. A greenhouse, coldframe, or hot bed are the traditional places to keep seeded flats, but an enclosed porch, a sunny window, or any other light, sheltered place is fine.

Transplanting is the only drawback to seeding in flats. Some plants can't withstand the shock of transplanting and die from it; the growth of other plants is greatly slowed by transplanting. (These problems can usually be avoided if you plant in small pots or planting cubes made of peat moss or other organic material instead of the standard wooden flats. The pots or cubes are set in the ground when the plants are large enough and slowly decompose as the roots expand.)

When to sow. Since you can control the environment of plants in flats, you aren't restricted to planting dates

WOODEN FLAT or any low container is good for starting seeds. Sift soil through screen to remove lumps.

PLACE SEEDS carefully in shallow furrows made in soil with a ruler and cover lightly with soil.

defined by the weather. It takes between 2½ and 4 months for most annuals started from seed in flats to bloom, and you'll want to start the seeds so that they'll be ready to set out several weeks before you want flowers. Don't start seeds too early in the winter, since once the plants begin to mature they should be set out where they have room to spread and grow.

Soil preparation. The soil you use for starting seeds in flats should be loose, drain well (not cake like clay), and yet hold moisture. Good commercial starting mediums—such as perlite and vermiculite—are available at nurseries. If you want to mix your own starting soil, try equal parts of coarse river sand, leaf mold or peat moss, and garden soil. Screen this mixture through a ¼-inch wire mesh to eliminate lumps. To prevent damping off disease (a soil fungus that attacks seeds and tiny seedlings), treat the soil with a commercial fungicide and/or pour a small amount of the fungicide powder into the seed packet and shake it so that the seeds become coated.

How to sow. Fill the container to ½ inch of the top with soil mix and firm it down with a block of wood or the palm of your hand. Mark off rows 2 inches apart with a pencil or by pressing a ruler ⅛ to ¼ inch into the mix.

Carefully sprinkle the seeds in the furrows and cover them not more than ¼ inch deep with the soil mix. Firm the seeds down so that they are in good contact with the soil, then label the rows or flats carefully.

Water the flat or container with a fine mist to prevent disturbing the seeds. Or soak the bottom of the container in a sink or large basin full of water—the soil will absorb the water, and you avoid dislodging the seeds.

Cover the container with dampened newspaper and place it in a warm spot, out of direct sunlight (or in morning sun only for warmth). Keep the soil moist but not soaking wet by spraying with a very fine mist or by soaking the bottom of the container in a basin. If the soil was thoroughly moistened at the time of seeding, you may not find it necessary to water again until the seedlings appear. Check the container daily to make sure the soil hasn't dried out and to see whether the seeds have begun to sprout.

When the seeds sprout. As soon as the first seeds begin to come up, remove the covering of newspaper and move the container into a brighter, open location where the plants will receive filtered sunlight but still be protected from direct sun, cold weather, and wind.

Pricking out. When the tiny seedlings have two sets of true leaves, they should be "pricked out" or moved into a container that provides more growing space. First fill the new flats (they should be deeper than the starting flats) with a richer soil than the one used to start the seeds. A good commercial potting mix, available at the nursery, will be fine. If you mix your own soil, try 2 parts garden soil, 1 part river sand, and 1 part sifted peat moss.

Lift out small clumps of seedlings with a flat spatula as you would lift fried eggs from a pan. Be sure to lift the entire plant and its roots, being careful not to break or cut the roots. Separate the seedlings from one another, keeping each root system intact, and set them in the new container about 1½ inches apart in holes large enough for the roots of the seedlings. Gently firm the soil around the roots. After moving the plants into the new container, water them thoroughly with a fine spray and place them in light shade for a couple of days.

When growing seedlings that will have different colored flowers, be sure to transplant the smaller seedlings along with the larger, more vigorous ones as some colors do not grow as fast and are slower to mature than others.

Keep the seedlings watered, gradually exposing them to more and more sun each day. This way, by the time they're ready to set out in the garden—4 to 5 weeks—they can take full sun all day without wilting.

Transplanting to the garden. Once your flat-grown seedlings are ready to withstand living outdoors all day and night, you can transplant them into their permanent garden home. Always transplant carefully, since flat-grown seedlings can suffer a setback or even fatality if mishandled.

BUYING NURSERY PLANTS

Buying young plants from the nursery (available during the growing season) is the most convenient way for many gardeners to get their annuals, especially those who don't have the time or garden space for starting their own plants from seeds and gardeners who want just a dozen or so plants for containers or a small border.

You'll find annual plants being sold at nurseries in several different ways. Two of the most common are in wooden flats and in low plastic containers divided into sections like an egg carton. In both cases, they are usually sold by the dozen or half-dozen. Another way you might find plants is growing in 4 or 6-inch plastic pots—one or two plants in each pot.

Since flats and sectioned plastic containers do not allow enough room for roots to expand and develop fully, you should choose only very young plants in these containers and pass up plants that are in bloom or bud since they may not give you the best performance.

Four or six-inch plastic pots, on the other hand, are usually large enough for the roots to grow and develop. You may find plants in these pots that are already in bloom or bud. They are an excellent choice for instant color.

If you do decide to buy nursery plants, here are some tips on selecting healthy plants capable of giving you the most for your money:

● Look for full-foliaged, compact little plants. A well-branched small plant usually has a larger, stronger root system than a tall, leggy one.

● Foliage is a good indication of a plant's health and vigor. Strong plants have leaves that feel crisp and are a fresh green color with no yellowing or browning at the edges. Drooping leaves may indicate weak plants grown without enough water, air, or light—or perhaps they were frost-nipped.

● When buying seedlings by the dozen, see that they are removed from the flat carefully; keep soil packed around their roots. Feeder roots exposed to air will quickly dry out, giving plants a crippling setback. Keep plants shaded and well watered until you are ready to transplant.

TRANSPLANTING

Plants that you've bought from the nursery or grown from seeds in flats will need to be transplanted either into your garden or into a permanent container. Transplanting is crucial because the plants and their roots must become adjusted to an entirely new environment—soil, temperature, sun, and water. Even if the roots aren't damaged in transplanting and you take every precaution, it still takes time and strength for plants to regain their equilibrium. To avoid bad luck and get your plants off to a good start, follow the instructions below.

● Prepare the soil before you transplant. The soil

YOUNG ANNUALS sold at nurseries in flats or plastic "6-packs" (above) should be compact, full-foliaged.

TO PLANT annuals bought from the nursery or raised in flats, first dig a hole large enough for the plant's root ball.

HOLD plant in the hole so the top of root ball is slightly lower than soil level, fill in around the roots with soil.

should be prepared as thoroughly as it would if you were starting seeds. See pages 7–8 for instructions on soil conditioning and preparation. After preparing the soil, water it thoroughly before transplanting so that roots can receive water as soon as they are in the ground.

• Transplant under favorable conditions. Try to avoid transplanting on hot days and particularly during the mid-afternoon. The heat and sun may absorb moisture from the plants or may wilt them before the roots have a chance to replenish lost water. Cloudy and foggy days, early morning, and late afternoon are the ideal times to plant.

• Dig generous planting holes. Planting holes should be large enough for the roots to grow outward into loose soil rather than have to strain through packed soil. Cut the sides of the hole vertically with a trowel and work up the soil in the bottom of the hole to make a soft cushion for the roots.

• Lift plants carefully. When you dig the small plants out of the flats, try to keep as much soil as possible around the roots. This is easiest if the soil is damp. Separate the plants as though you were cutting a pan of brownies and lift them out with a spatula or putty knife; don't use a trowel.

• Set in the plant. Place the plant in the hole slightly lower than level with the ground. Fill in around it with well-pulverized soil mixed with fertilizer, leaving a shallow basin around the stem for water. Except with African marigolds (see page 44), be careful not to place soil around the stem.

• Water thoroughly. You may find it helpful to add some liquid vitamin B-1 to the first watering; this

PLANTS removed from nursery containers may be root-bound: loosen the roots with your fingers before planting.

vitamin lessens the shock of transplanting and encourages root development.

● Shade if necessary. If the weather is hot, shade the transplants from direct sun for a couple of days with cardboard, burlap, or newspapers supported on stakes or bent into a tent shape. A good-sized portable lath frame is the best solution. Make one by tacking laths (about an inch apart) to a rectangular frame of 1 by 2s with a length of 2 by 4 nailed to each corner.

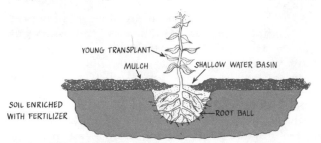

TRANSPLANT off to a good start: planting hole large enough for root ball; loose soil allows easy root spread; mulch prevents soil from drying out too rapidly.

CARE FOR YOUR ANNUALS

Small plants, like small children, need more care and attention than adult plants. Once you've nurtured your seedlings to the stage where they are beginning to bud, the most difficult work is over. But there are still things you'll need to do to keep the plants healthy and happily blooming: watering, weeding, mulching, controlling pests and diseases, and prolonging bloom.

Watering and feeding

Once your plants have begun to sprout, they'll do best if the soil's surface dries out slightly between waterings: this stimulates the roots to spread out and grow deeply. The trick in watering is to do it gently but thoroughly—gently so you don't flatten the plants or knock off their buds and thoroughly so that water gets down to the plant's roots. A two-minute hosing of the flower bed is not sufficient. You should water until the soil is thoroughly moistened for several inches below the surface.

Since watering from above the foliage can bend or break plants, you may want to flood the soil from below the plants. If you do water the plants from above, use a very fine spray and avoid moistening plants during midday or near sunset. (Hot midday sun can blister wet foliage; watering late in the day can encourage fungus disease to develop.) After a thorough watering, don't water again until the first inch of soil is dry. See page 9 for feeding instructions.

Weeding

The gardener's curse, weeds in a planting bed detract from the beauty of the flowers and rob them of nutrients and water. Your chore of removing weeds will begin as soon as they can be distinguished from the annual flowers you are cultivating and will continue until the end of the growing season.

Simply grabbing the stem and foliage of the impinging weed and yanking it out of the ground may seem the easiest method of weeding. If you pull up the root system, not just breaking off the stem at ground level, and do not disturb surrounding plants, this method is fine. But if the weeds are large, tough, and have strong, deep roots, you might have the best success if you use one of the many weeding tools available at hardware stores and nurseries. Usually, weeding tools have a short handle and a screwdriver-like blade with a notch or V in the tip. You use the tool like a crowbar, pushing the tip under and against the roots or stem of the weed and carefully prying upwards to lift the weed out, root and all.

Mulching

Mulches are coverings over the soil around plants that provide an insulation between the soil and air. They will help prevent the ground from drying out, keep the roots and soil at a fairly even temperature, and help hold down weeds.

Most mulches are organic materials—such as sawdust, compost or ground bark—that hold moisture well and can simply be turned under into the soil at the end of the growing season. Spread mulch an inch deep over the soil below and around plants.

As they decompose, some mulches (particularly raw sawdust and ground bark) can rob from your soil nitrogen that is needed by the plants. Be sure to use a mulch that has a high nitrogen content such as compost or nitrogen fortified ground bark or sawdust (available at most nurseries and garden centers).

Pests and diseases

Both organic and non-organic sprays and dusts are available to take care of just about any pest or disease that may come along. Some annuals, such as marigolds, are not only pest resistant themselves but also can give neighboring plants a degree of immunity to some pests. Check the label on the spray you buy to be sure it will work against the problem you have. Set out bait for snails and slugs (see page 9).

You may need a fungicide to combat mildew on such plants as calendulas, sweet peas, and zinnias. (Some hybrids have been developed that are mildew resistant; the results—especially in zinnias—are dramatic.) Mildew is a powdery white growth that is hard to control once it gets a foothold, so act quickly as soon as you notice it. If mildew is a problem in your area, you may want to avoid types of plants most likely to be vulnerable. Your nurseryman can offer advice if you are in doubt.

Prolonging bloom

The life cycle of annuals is to grow, flower, set seed, and die. There's a point in each plant's development when the tissues harden, growth stops, and the seed part of the cycle is triggered.

Hot weather hardens the tissues prematurely (this is why many annuals bloom longer in cool coastal gardens than they will in hot inland gardens). Tissues also harden if the supply of nutrients gives out before the plant matures. Cold nights and drying winds will also cause tissues to harden, as will lack of water and damage to the plant by disease and certain pests.

Whatever you can do to prevent premature hardening of the plant tissues will prolong bloom—protection from extreme heat and cold, regular watering and feeding. Even after natural hardening has started, you can encourage more flowers to develop simply by removing the faded blossoms or by cutting the flowers frequently for your house to prevent the development of seeds. As long as there are enough nutrients in the soil, your plants will keep trying to replace the lost flowers until the final hardening begins. Be sure to feed your plants as described on page 9.

Once the plants have hardened and begin going to seed, they will no longer be an asset to your garden. Eventually you'll just have to be ruthless and pull them out, especially if you want to make room for late-blooming annuals, perennials, shrubs, or bulbs.

If you've found pleasure in the annuals that you've grown, you can save the seeds for next year. Simply shake the seeds out of the flower heads and let them dry thoroughly. Put them in paper packets until next year. Unless you really enjoy surprises, label the packets carefully; you may not remember which is which next spring.

COMMERCIAL GARDENING AIDS

Many commercial products are available at nurseries and garden supply stores that not only will make seed growing and transplanting easier but also will help assure healthy, long-blooming plants.

Perhaps the biggest time and work saver is premixed potting soil available in sacks at the nursery. The soil can be used for potting and transplanting almost all annuals and saves you from mixing your own ideal soil from scratch.

Small pots made of compressed peat moss, manure, or other organic material are excellent containers for starting seeds. You fill the pots with starting mix or potting soil and put several seeds in each. When the plants are large enough for the garden, you avoid the step of transplanting, which ordinarily retards growth; instead, you just set the pot and plant in the ground together. The pot slowly decomposes as the roots of the plants expand. Humus pots are especially helpful for growing hard-to-transplant seeds.

Similar to peat pots are compressed peat moss cubes. The cubes are about ½ inch thick when you purchase them and swell up to about 1½ inches thick when moistened with water. All you do is press two or three seeds into one side of each moistened cube. The seeds germinate quickly, and the seedings will be ready to transplant into the garden when the roots begin showing through the sides of the cube. When planting, be sure to cover the entire root ball (inside the cube) with soil.

One thing you should be aware of when using peat pots and planting cubes is that they tend to dry out quickly. You should take extra care in watering regularly, being sure to water *within* the pot (or over the cube), as well as around it. Make between-watering checks for drying.

Seed tapes are helpful when you plant very fine seeds in the garden. The seeds are embedded the correct distance apart in a thin fibrous tape or sheet. All you do is plant the tape or sheet in the garden and water; the fiber protects the seeds from birds during the germination period and retains moisture to prevent drying out. (The soil must still be well prepared, just as it does for regular seeding.)

Seeds for the more popular annuals are often available in small flats that contain seed, soil, and nutrients. All you need to do is remove the lid or punch holes in it then water it. Some of these kits have a plastic lid and even a lighting cable that creates a greenhouse environment for quickest germination. The flats are usually made of a humus material and are divided

PEAT POTS are ideal for starting seeds; when roots begin growing through sides, plant is ready for garden.

INTO THE GARDEN go peat pot and plant. Just prepare soil and set pot in hole. Always water within pot rim.

into sections. When the plants are ready for the garden, you just separate the sections and put them into the ground. The sections will slowly decompose as the plants grow.

Many seeds come in pelleted form. Each seed is coated with a material that disintegrates when the pellets are planted and watered. The added bulk of the seeds makes them easy to see and handle—a boon when you want even spacing. The coatings often contain fungicides to prevent diseases, and some are dyed to indicate flower color. When using pelleted seeds be sure to keep the soil moist as the pelleting material has a tendency to absorb moisture while the seeds themselves remain dry.

ANNUALS AS CUT FLOWERS

Most annuals make excellent cut flowers for indoor arrangements and bouquets. Under the individual descriptions in the encyclopedia (pages 24-63), you'll find information and suggestions for cutting and arranging the suitable flowers. Below are some general rules for the care of cut flowers that should help keep your arrangements fresh and attractive for the longest possible time:

When to cut flowers. The best time to cut flowers is in the early morning or in the cool of the evening. Never cut flowers from plants that are dry; water

thoroughly a few hours before you intend to pick.

How to cut flowers. A sharp knife is the best tool for cutting flowers; scissors and pruning shears tend to crush the stem cells through which water is admitted. Make long, slanting cuts to increase the amount of surface that will be exposed to water. With larger, heavier stems, cut a slit about an inch up from the end of the stem. Cut the stems as long as possible; shorten them as necessary when making up the arrangement.

For more interesting bouquets, pick flowers in different stages of development—in full bloom, partly opened, and in bud. If the foliage is attractive, cut some to add to the bouquet.

After cutting. Immediately after cutting, place the flowers in a deep container filled with cold water. Some gardeners carry a pail of water with them into the garden and place each stem in it as they cut. For maximum longevity, let the flowers stand in deep water for several hours or even overnight.

Special treatments. Certain flowers, such as poppies, lose sap from their stems after being cut. To prevent the water-conducting tubes in the stems from becoming clogged by the sap, seal the cut ends by searing them in a flame or dipping them in boiling water for a couple of seconds. If you place them in water right after treatment, these flowers will keep fresh for several days.

Arranging. When it's time to arrange the flowers, be sure to strip the leaves from the part of the stem that will be under water; otherwise, they'll discolor the water and smell terribly. Arrange the flowers so that they have room to breathe and so oxygen can reach the water.

Daily care. Cut flowers prefer rooms at a temperature of about 50°; people like rooms warmer. Even in a fairly warm room, most cut flowers should remain in good condition for several days if you follow these steps:

● Recut stems once a day. This will remove the bacteria that develops on the cut surface of the stem.

● Remove faded flowers promptly to keep the arrangement looking fresh and tidy and to make room for buds that may be ready to unfold.

● If you can possibly do it, change the water in the container daily to cut down on bacteria and odor. If you can't change the water, add fresh water to replace what has evaporated.

● Keep arrangements out of drafts, direct sunlight, and blasts of hot air.

● Some people feel that additives to the water prolong the life of cut flowers. These range from folk remedies, such as copper pennies and aspirin, to commercial products. Most professional arrangers, though, feel that following the steps outlined above is more helpful than anything else.

Annuals in Action

The new look: you can give it to your house through furniture and fresh paint, to your personal appearance through clothing, and to your garden through planting annuals. Annuals, however, are far less expensive than clothing and furniture, and planting them is much easier than painting the house.

A unique feature of annuals is that you plant them afresh each season and remove them from the garden when they begin to fade. Growing annuals frees you not only from year-round garden maintenance and responsibility but also from a permanent landscape plan. Each time you plant you can create an entirely new garden or give fresh appeal to permanent garden features such as shrubs, walks, and fences.

Planning and consideration before you plant is the best assurance of getting the most satisfaction from your annuals. On the following pages are suggestions and ideas for using flower color effectively, for combining annuals and other plants, for solving landscape problems with annuals, and for growing annuals in containers.

COLOR WITH ANNUALS

Flower color can enhance your garden in many ways. A single color massed in borders can lend its tone to the entire garden, small plantings (perhaps in containers) offer brilliant highlights to permanent plantings or the patio, and combined plantings of several different colors will provide endless variety and excitement.

As in selecting furniture or a shirt and tie, the flowers you choose to grow and where you decide to plant them depend on your personal tastes and preferences. But however you use color in the garden, three basic color relationships—harmony, contrast, and subordination—may help you create the effects you want, give you new planting ideas, or help you make that favorite flower really shine.

Harmony

Looking at the color wheel on page 18, notice how similar the tones between each pair of primary colors (red, yellow, and blue) appear to be. Actually these colors are graduated mixtures of the adjacent primary colors and very closely related. (You may also see that each color is graduated in tone—these shades are created by adding black or white to the pure shade which appears in the large center band in the wheel.)

The closer together two or more colors are on the color wheel, the less difference there is between them. When similar colors appear in a combination, they seem to flow together—an effect known as harmony.

Two harmonious color combinations that frequently appear in gardens are those involving "hot" colors such as yellow, orange, and red and "cool" colors—blue, green, and violet. The overall effect of these harmonies on the garden is to give it a warm or cool feeling.

Another effective way of using harmony is in interplantings and edgings that provide variety and relief yet still maintain the feeling of a single-color mass planting.

Contrast

Colors that lie opposite one another on the color wheel (yellow and violet for instance) are complementary. Unlike harmonious colors, complementary colors contrast with each other and your eye jumps quickly from one to the other.

In complementary combinations each color takes on a much crisper, richer tone than it has alone. Thus, green foliage or out-of-season shrubs will appear lusher and cooler when contrasted with a splash of red, and a container of yellow marigolds will be even more vibrant if given an edging of blue.

Subordination

Just as too much harmony can become dull and repetitive, too much contrast can make a garden appear busy, confusing, and uncoordinated. When planting combinations of colors, one way of assuring success is to keep a single color dominant and the other colors subordinate to it.

In both harmonious and complementary combinations, a dominating color provides a point of focus and stability. While subordinate colors offer variety and/or contrast, attention will always return to the dominant color for rest and relief.

COMBINING ANNUALS IN THE LANDSCAPE

In combining annuals and other plants in the garden or containers, you'll not only want to consider the effects of color but also growth form. For example, by planting low growing plants in front of taller ones or combining spreading plants with more upright types, you give the garden a feeling of movement and coordination.

Below are some effective combinations of annuals and other plants that you might like to try. Some of the combinations can be adapted on a small scale to containers:

● Blue petunias with blue ageratum and lobelia.
● One color in a border through an entire season—for example, yellows: calendulas and yellow violas for the cool months of late winter and spring; marigolds or zinnias for summer and fall.
● A round bed filled with maroon, plumy celosias surrounded by orange marigolds, with an edging of blue ageratum.
● Dwarf citrus with *Sedum praealtum* and orange or yellow calendulas or dwarf marigolds.
● Old-fashioned lavender heliotrope with purple petunias.
● Purple sweet alyssum edging around a wide band of dwarf yellow marigolds, the center filled with white petunias.
● Pink snapdragons with a border of pink and white sweet alyssum.
● Dwarf yellow marigolds as a border for magenta globe amaranth.
● Rose beds edged with annual pinks *(Dianthus)* and sweet alyssum.
● Crimson bougainvillea on a trellis underplanted with blue ageratum and deep purple petunias.
● Red salvia border against a background of tall, soft yellow marigolds or white zinnias.
● A bed of white petunias with islands of pink or purple petunias, each island consisting of about three plants.
● Pink sweet alyssum woven between blue lobelia, blue viola, purple nierembergia, or blue ageratum.
● Yellow and apricot gladiolus with yellow, apricot, and bronze snapdragons. For contrast, add a group of brilliant blue Chinese forget-me-nots.
● Mixed nicotiana in pink, red, and white behind impatiens or torenia.
● In the background, deep rose-colored cosmos; next interplanted pink or white cleome with an edging of pink or white petunias.
● Lavender and purple stock as a background for pale blue lace flowers. In front, double-flowered dwarf balsam in shades of pink and rose-red and white.
● Yellow hollyhocks, blue larkspur, and blue cornflower with pale salmon-pink godetia or salmon-rose dwarf zinnia.

THE VERSATILE ANNUALS

Most gardeners are limited to what they can plant by permanent garden features, such as fences and walks, or by fixed natural conditions, such as sun and shade. Other gardeners may need a particular plant to fill a need—covering large amounts of ground or filling a difficult corner that is in need of brightening. Below are some common garden situations and ideas for planting them.

Small garden borders

In many small gardens where planting space is limited, flowers must often be confined to borders or strips (usually 3 to 4 feet wide). Such borders not only can be gay and lively for several months but also can provide cut flowers.

Single plantings for these borders are often a solution. You might try two rows of marigolds—a dwarf variety in front and a taller type in back—if the border is sunny (orange and yellow might be a good harmony of colors). Another idea would be to plant mixed petunias for both contrast and harmony in a sunny border. If the border is shady, try impatiens, mixed nicotiana, or mixed cineraria.

For an interesting effect with several different annuals and colors, plant penstemons 15 to 18 inches apart; then, every 3 or 4 feet, interplant annual white baby's breath. If the border is 4 feet wide or more, you'll have room to plant a row of dwarf Chinese delphinium (the deep blue variety gives the most striking effect) in front, with some white sweet alyssum directly along the edge. The baby's breath will raise its airy flowers slightly higher than the penstemons, just as it would in a bouquet.

Other plants to try in small borders might be cosmos, green and white-leafed snow-on-the-mountain, and pink or rose annual phlox.

Fence planting

A tall redwood or cedar fence or a white wall will provide a good setting for the spectacular reddish orange daisy flowers of tithonia (variously called Mexican sunflower, tree zinnia, and golden flower of the Incas), red and orange zinnias, and scarlet and gold salpiglossis. Don't leave too little space for this sunloving combination—tithonias will grow to 8 feet tall and spread out to 6 feet.

For a fence planting in several colors, sow seed of morning glory directly against the fence; in front, plant orange zinnias, edged by dwarf yellow marigolds.

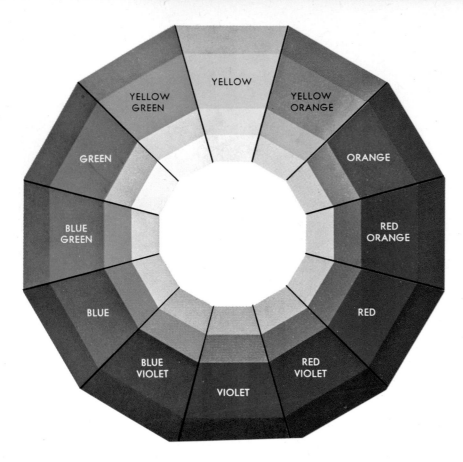

THE COLOR WHEEL *shows the relationships between colors. Colors in between the primary colors (red, yellow, blue) are created by mixing together different amounts of the primary colors on either side. Colors close together on the wheel are similar and tend to blend together in a harmony; opposite colors contrast with each other. Adding black or white to a color darkens or lightens it; pure colors appear in the center band in the wheel.*

FLOWER COLOR IN ACTION. **Top right:** *blue lobelia and yellow marigolds are a striking contrast.* **Above:** *red and violet petunias illustrate the subtle transitions created through harmonious color plantings.* **Right:** *red and white impatiens gives contrasting warmth to green foliage but doesn't overpower its dominant cool tone.*

Ground covers

Low-growing annuals make ideal ground covers between newly planted shrubs and trees that have not yet become well established and filled out to full size. In large gardens, the best solution is to scatter seed of wild flowers or seeds of an easy annual, such as alyssum. For a stunning effect, sow a ground cover of pink sweet alyssum around pink or white Floribunda roses.

Annuals as problem solvers

Here are some common garden problems and a few of the annuals that will help you solve them. Keep one thing in mind: these recommendations are not intended to put a halter on your imagination; dozens of other excellent annuals will do the same job.

Bare spots in bulb beds. If you grow bulbs, you have the problem of what to do for color when the flowers are gone and the foliage begins to fade. Annuals planted at this time will fill in as the bulb foliage withers. They will also leave the ground free for working with the bulbs in the fall and spring. Choose annuals that are adapted to the bulb's cultural requirements. Marigold, zinnia, and poppy are a few good choices for sunny spots; try cineraria, lobelia, or Madagascar periwinkle in shade or semi-shade.

Sparse look of new shrub plantings. When you start a foundation planting, shrub border, or hedge, the planting may look quite bare for the first year or so. Use annuals for temporary fillers. Choose bushy types, such as snapdragons and stock, that won't spread and take over the planting.

Lack of color in shrub borders. Annuals can do a great deal to keep a shrub border interesting after its flowers have faded. Choose vigorous plants that carry bloom high enough to be seen—larkspur, nicotiana, salpiglossis, cosmos, cleome, hollyhock, or foxglove are good choices. Among the best edging and border plants are annuals. Some are neat and formal; others are more casual. Try sweet alyssum, nemesia, dwarf marigold (formal), petunia, or annual phlox (informal).

Difficult dry locations. Large lots and country places often have corners or sections that are difficult to water. What you need in these places are annuals that manage very well with minimum watering or occasional rainfall, and perhaps thrive in full sun. Try verbena, nasturtium, or portulaca.

Fast-growing vines

Vines that grow from seed to maturity in a hurry can give an immediate, spectacular effect, covering very large areas inside of 6 or 8 weeks. They serve as fast, inexpensive fillers while you plan permanent plantings. Or they may give you shade from the hot afternoon sun during summer and leave the area open for sun during the winter. You might want to train the vine up a fence or wall for a vertical display of color to soften otherwise harsh lines and surfaces.

Some of the most popular and useful vines are sweet pea, morning glory (also effective for covering an unsightly steep bank), scarlet runner bean, trailing types of nasturtium, and cardinal climber.

ANNUALS IN CONTAINERS

Because most annuals adapt very well to the confines of pots, boxes, or hanging baskets, you'll find containers to be the perfect solution if you have limited space in the garden, want bright splashes of color on the terrace or patio, or plan to grow your flowers indoors.

Potting an annual

To pot a plant, first put a square of fine screen or a piece of broken pottery over the drainage hole in the bottom of the container to prevent it from clogging. Fill the container with potting soil (use either commercially mixed soil or a mix of one part garden soil, one part river sand, and one part vermiculite or perlite) until the plant will sit with the top of its root ball about an inch beneath the rim of the pot. Remove the plant from its nursery container or flat, set it in the container, then gently firm soil around its sides until level with the top of the root ball.

Watering and feeding

The greatest difference between container and open-ground gardening is in watering and feeding. In containers, the soil and roots are exposed to drying air on all sides, and water draining through the soil leaches out nutrients, so you'll need to water and feed plants in containers more frequently than those growing in the garden.

Just how often you should water and feed container plants depends on the plant and the growing conditions: no fixed schedule can be prescribed. A good rule of thumb is to water whenever the top inch of soil feels dry when you wiggle your finger in it.

Apply water to the soil from beneath the foliage, and always water thoroughly—until excess runs out the drainage hole in the bottom of the container. This assures water of getting all the way down to the roots where it is needed most.

Once you become familiar with your plant's needs by feeling the soil every day and watering when it is dry, you will probably develop a watering schedule. But don't let a routine prevent you from checking the plant between waterings: on an especially hot or windy day, the soil can quickly dry out, whereas during a cool spell you might not need to water as frequently.

OUT OF SEASON bulb foliage is livened by single-flowered French marigolds and ageratum.

VARIETY is one way to liven small borders. Here are verbenas (foreground), gazania (yellow), salvia, alyssum.

CALIFORNIA POPPIES readily naturalize, and provide easy color in sunny borders, parking strips.

DRIFTS OF BABY-BLUE-EYES form an attractive cover for bulbs such as these Dutch iris.

MASSED IN A BORDER and edged with lobelia, salpiglossis gives a rich variety of summer color.

*CAREFREE SPLASHES (left) of red, white, and blue, provided by plume celosia, phlox, and lobelia, liven border. **Above:** snapdragons can rise up into green foliage for a colorful accent.*

MASSES OF COLOR are provided by marigolds, petunias, and zinnias in this flower garden.

Like watering, feeding depends on the needs of the plant rather than on a fixed schedule. In general, frequent but light feeding is a better routine than infrequent but heavy feeding. Either liquid or dry commercial fertilizer will do; just be sure to follow the instructions on the label of the fertilizer you use.

Many fertilizers contain strong chemicals that can burn the roots of a plant if applied to the soil in large amounts. If you use liquid fertilizer, be careful not to get any on the plant's foliage and rinse off any that does since it may cause burning.

Selecting a container

Clay and ceramic pots, hanging planters, and wooden boxes and tubs are all available at nurseries and garden centers in many shapes, sizes, and colors. You can also adapt as planters any other sorts of container that will hold soil. Just be sure that any container you choose has a hole or slot for excess water to drain from. Excess water, unless allowed to drain, will waterlog the soil at the bottom of a container, preventing air from reaching the roots and causing root rot or other diseases.

Most containers fall into two categories: porous and nonporous. Porous containers include those made of unglazed clay and some untreated woods—any material that water and air can penetrate. Nonporous containers are those made of materials through which water and air can't penetrate—metal, glazed clay, and some finished woods. You'll need to water the plants in porous containers more often than those in nonporous ones, but you must be more careful to provide adequate drainage and soil aeration (by using a loose soil mix) for plants in nonporous containers.

If you plan to put a container indoors or on an outdoor surface (such as brick) that might be stained by water that drains out, put a dish or saucer beneath it to catch the drainage. Be sure to empty the dish after watering so that soil in the bottom of the container won't become waterlogged.

Twenty container favorites

Though most annuals can be grown in containers, below are 20 plants that many gardeners find outstanding container specimens:

Ageratum. Combine dwarf varieties with petunias or annual phlox or interplant with white or pink sweet alyssum.

Alyssum. All varieties of sweet alyssum make quick and effective ground covers or edgings for taller plants in containers. Sow seeds in the container or set out plants from flats.

Browallia. One of the best for long lasting summer and fall color in partial shade. Attractive in groupings with tuberous begonias, fuchsias, and hydrangeas.

Butterfly flower. Pastel-flowered plants are charming alone or with fairy primrose, cinerarias, or blue or white violas.

Cineraria. When well grown, this is a spectacular container plant for shady outdoor areas in frost-free climates. Group with pots of browallia, coleus, lobelia, or nicotiana.

Coleus. The colorful foliage of coleus brightens patios and terraces in the summer. It is also a very popular house plant. Provide sufficient but indirect light.

Dianthus. For a fresh, jaunty effect, surround a pot or boxful of dianthus with an edging of 'Carpet of Snow' sweet alyssum.

Fairy primrose. In mild climates, this is one of the most effective plants for spring color in containers. Try with daffodils, hyacinths, tulips, and other bulbs.

Impatiens. Both *I. holstii* and *I. sultanii* are fine container plants for partial shade during the summer and early fall months.

Lobelia. Perfect for containers, particularly as an accompaniment to other plants.

Marigold. Dwarf varieties are especially serviceable, long-blooming container plants.

Mignonette. If you want fragrance close by, grow mignonette in a pot or box near an open window; breezes will bring their sweetness indoors. Sow seed directly in the container.

Mimulus. An unusually pretty flower to grace shaded areas of a patio.

Nasturtium. Among the easiest annuals to grow in pots. Sow the seeds directly in the container, then thin to the desired number of plants.

Nicotiana. White nicotiana is especially appealing for its fragrance and cool appearance on summer evenings.

Petunia. Invaluable for all kinds of containers. Trailing varieties are outstanding in hanging baskets. Dwarf and medium height types are fine in pots or boxes.

Phlox. Set annual phlox rather thickly in boxes, tubs, or large pots. Dwarf varieties are most satisfactory since they are less inclined to sprawl.

Torenia. Dainty plant for close-up containers in partial shade. Combine with light and dark blue lobelia.

Viola. As useful for spring and early summer color in containers as it is in the ground. Blue or white violas are compatible with almost anything.

Virginian stock. For a multi-colored carpet under taller annuals or beneath shrubs and trees in wooden tubs and planters.

FOR PYRAMID, stack pots, then plant open areas.

MOSS-LINED BASKETS are perfect for alyssum and violas.

*CONTAINERS (left) are the answer if you have no ground space. Marigolds, alyssum, cosmos (foreground) are effective in masses. **Above:** lobelia makes a perfect container groundcover for bright yellow marigolds.*

A Parade of Favorites: African Daisy to Zinnia

One of the intriguing things about annuals (and plants in general) is that, like people, each is an individual. On the following pages, over 75 of the most popular and widely available annuals are presented in detail. Along with the description of each plant, you'll find information on its culture requirements, tips on growing it from seeds or nursery plants, planting times, and ideas for using it in the landscape, in containers, or as cut flowers.

The plants are listed in alphabetical order under the names they are commonly known by. Beneath the common name you'll find the plant's botanical name (except when it is the same as the common name), other frequently used common names, and a reference to the page where its color photograph can be found.

Not all of the plants listed are true annuals. Some are biennials that flower during the first year they are planted. Others are tender perennials that live over from one year to the next only in ideal climates and are treated as annuals elsewhere, being replanted each year for fresh bloom.

African Daisy

Dimorphotheca (Cape marigold). Photo on page 26.

Since their blossoms open only in full sun and close at night and on cloudy days, plenty of sunshine is the main requirement for successful African daisies. Fine for cutting, the glossy, daisylike flowers come in mixed colors of apricot, rose, salmon, white, and yellow and in white with a blue-black center ringed with blue. Plants grow 6 to 12 inches high and spread into solid mounds. Mass them in flower beds or parking strips or use them to edge a walk. African daisies thrive on the heat from a reflecting wall or fence, require only light watering, and need no special care.

In warm climates such as the Southwest's low desert areas, African daisies put on a fine show of bloom during winter and early spring. There plants often become so covered with blossoms that the foliage is hardly visible. In more humid regions, lush foliage and fewer blooms are produced.

In mild climates, where winter temperatures generally stay above 25°, broadcast seeds outdoors in late summer so plants will be in bud before cold weather arrives. If you live in a cool but dry area with severe winters, plant seeds outdoors in the spring when the soil is warm for a good show of blooms from late summer until heavy frost.

Species and varieties include *D. sinuata* (usually sold as *D.* 'Aurantiaca'): daisylike, 2½-inch flowers on 1-foot-high plants; and *D. pluvialis* 'Ringens' (available under the nursery name *D.* 'Hybrida Ringens'): 6 to 8-inch plants with white 4-inch flowers.

Ageratum

Ageratum houstonianum (Floss flower).
Photo on page 26.

For a dependable, long-blooming swatch of soft blue in your garden, ageratum is a fine choice. From early summer until frost, ageratum is continuously covered with clustered heads of tiny, silky, fringed flowers in dusty shades of lavender-blue, lavender-pink, or white. The popular dwarf varieties grow in mounds 6 to 12 inches high and 12 inches across; they make fine container plants. Larger types grow up to 3 feet tall. Ageratum makes an excellent edging.

Since seedlings grow slowly and remain small for weeks, sowing ageratum seeds directly in the garden after frosts is usually disappointing. You may prefer to buy your plants from the nursery. If you do decide to grow ageratum from seed, germinate them indoors in flats, 8 weeks prior to the first frost-free date (see page 7).

Plant ageratum in good, well-drained soil; water regularly. It prefers full sun, but where summers are long and hot, ageratum does best on the east side of the house or in other light shade. Planted in poor soil and not given enough water, ageratum may turn brown, especially if the weather is hot. To bring back these plants, water heavily, feed once a month, and remove the dead flower heads.

Popular dwarf varieties include 'Fairy Pink,' a very dwarf form with large flower clusters; 'Blue Chip' and 'Blue Mink,' larger dwarfs; and 'Blue Blazer,' which is a blue-flowered dwarf. 'Summer Snow,' an F_1 hybrid, is a white variety.

Alyssum, sweet

Lobularia maritima. Photo on page 26.

In sweet-smelling drifts of white, violet, or rose-colored flowers, low and lacy sweet alyssum is an ideal edging plant and a perfect fast-growing ground cover. It also makes a perfect low-growing container plant.

Each plant puts up a number of irregular, 2 to 6-inch-high stalks, bearing slender green leaves and a bouquet of tiny, ¼-inch, four-petalled flowers. White-flowered types are very popular because they set off every garden color so well, but varieties with violet and rose-colored flowers are pretty with violas or dianthus.

Sweet alyssum (the regular alyssum is a perennial) is hardy and sun-loving, does well in ordinary garden soil, and requires little attention. It is a fast grower (six weeks from seed to flower) and blooms from earliest spring to late fall—even through winter in mild areas.

You can buy sweet alyssum seeds in packets and broadcast them in the garden where plants are to grow during spring or fall. (Summer seeding is generally not satisfactory.) Plan on about a week for the seeds to germinate if the soil is warm—a little longer if it's cool and wet. An alternative to growing alyssum from seed is to purchase your plants from the nursery. Sweet alyssum needs only light watering and, while it does best in the sun, will tolerate partial shade.

Varieties: 'Carpet of Snow,' 'Royal Carpet,' and 'Rosie O'Day' are dwarf varieties (2 to 4 inches high) with white, violet, and lavender-pink flowers respectively.

Amaranthus

Amaranthus species. Photo on page 26.

Spectacular in size and vivid in color, amaranthus is an eye-catcher in any garden. A huge, untidy plant with coarse showy leaves, amaranthus can spread to cover 4 square feet and will reach 3 to 6 feet in height. If you have the garden space and live in a climate with a long, hot growing season, you might try amaranthus as a background plant or mass it in a large planting bed against a fence or wall.

Since amaranthus does not transplant well, plant seeds in their permanent home during the spring when the soil is warm. Water and feed seedlings regularly only until they mature and their colors appear. Established plants need little or no water; the colors will last all summer.

In the most popular types, the foliage carries the color. *A. tricolor* 'Molten Fire' has leaves that turn incandescent red at maturity. Joseph's coat (*A. t. splendens*) has narrow leaves blotched with gold, green, and red. Love-lies-bleeding (*A. caudatus*) bears long spikes of drooping red flower tassels that can be dried and used in arrangements.

Anagallis

Anagallis linifolia. Photo on page 28.

Some people may know anagallis as a wildflower. The domesticated anagallis (*A. linifolia,* usually sold as *A. grandiflora*), grows to 18 inches high and has ¾-inch-wide,

saucer-shaped blue blossoms. It can be an asset in a rock garden or among drifts of sweet alyssum. A biennial or short-lived perennial grown as an annual, anagallis grows well in temperate northern or mountain climates and in cool areas of California, where it prefers sun.

SWEET ALYSSUM (foreground) spills onto patio and fills in around taller, loose-growing anagallis.

Sow seeds in 1-inch-deep garden furrows, which will serve as water troughs, as soon as the soil is dry enough to be worked in the spring. Soak the seeded bed with a fine spray of water. Seeds start slowly, taking 2 to 3 weeks to sprout, so cover them very lightly with soil.

Try anagallis in drifts with white sweet alyssum or snow-in-summer or place it among clumps of dusty miller.

Anchusa Capensis

(Cape forget-me-not). Photo on page 28.

This tall, sturdy South African forget-me-not puts forth blue blossoms that grace summer flower gardens. In general, anchusa is biennial, but two annual flowering varieties are available: 'Blue Bird,' 1½ to 2 feet tall, and 'Blue Angel,' a more compact dwarf growing 8 to 10 inches tall. Both varieties are vase-shaped with many slender, hairy, upright branches, topped by clusters of tiny flowers.

Sow anchusa seeds outdoors when the soil is warm and dry. Try chilling the seeds for 72 hours before planting for quickest germination and growth. Anchusa likes full sun but will tolerate partial shade. For maximum color, shear the plants after the first show of bloom, then feed and water regularly; they will come back fuller, with even more color.

Use anchusa in drifts among yellow or pink snapdragons or behind an edging of yellow marigolds or white petunias.

Aster

Callistephus chinensis (China aster). Photo on page 28.

Here is your cutting flower! You can choose from flowers with quilled, curled, in-curved, ribbonlike, or interlaced rays and some with crested centers. The flowers are 2 to 3 inches across and come in single or mixed colors of crimson, pink, purple, rose, and white. They bloom all summer long, and, when cut, the blossoms last for a week or more.

(Continued on page 27)

AGERATUM

SWEET ALYSSUM

AFRICAN DAISY

AMARANTHUS

(Continued from page 25)

Tall varieties have thin, wiry, 1¼ to 3-foot stems that sometimes bend under the weight of the blooms; they tend to be leggy and look best in a bed backed and bordered by other flowers. Dwarfs are sturdier; growing 8 to 10 inches high, they can make attractive edging plants.

Asters have big seeds that sprout quickly; seedlings transplant with little fuss. If the frost-free season in your area is shorter than 5 months, start asters from seeds indoors in flats, 8 weeks prior to the frost-free date (see page 7). Otherwise, plant seeds outdoors in full sun.

Two problems common with asters are aster yellows and aster wilt. Aster yellows is caused by a virus carried by sucking insects and can make plants yellow and die. Dust or spray to repel the virus-carrying insects. Once infected, plants can't be treated, and should be removed.

Aster wilt is a fungus carried in the soil. Prevent it from infecting plants by planting only wilt-resistant aster types. Overwatering increases the chance of disease. To give your plants the best chance of success, change the location of your aster bed each year or fumigate and treat the bed with a fungicide before planting.

Among the most interesting strains, Powderpuffs is a double-flowered, upright, 2-foot-high plant; Double Crego, 3 feet tall, has shaggy 3-inch blossoms with twisted rays; Perfection is a ball-type flower on 4 foot-stems; Dwarf Queen, an 8 to 12-inch plant, has double flowers.

Baby-Blue-Eyes

Nemophila menziesii, usually sold as *N. insignis.* Photo on page 28.

A spring-blooming Western native, baby-blue-eyes bears masses of clear blue, cup-shaped flowers on short fragile stems, 6 to 10 inches high. The blossoms, 1 to 1½ inches across with white centers, look best in drifts among daffodils or tulips, in rock gardens, or as an edging for other cool-loving, quick-blooming annuals such as nemesia or linaria. Baby-blue-eyes is very attractive in hanging baskets.

Baby-blue-eyes has a short blooming season, and you'll want to seed it in the fall or very early spring. Sow the seeds in moist soil that receives shade in the afternoon. Scatter seeds thickly: plants are dainty and fine leafed and should be spaced close enough for the foliage to fill in between the plants and shade the soil beneath. As cut flowers, baby-blue-eyes will last 2 or 3 days.

Baby's Breath

Gypsophila elegans. Photo on page 29.

Growing rapidly to 1 to 2 feet, baby's breath has criss-crossing stems bearing tiny, rounded, pearly white blossoms. In full bloom, the plants have the delicate, frothy lightness of a cloud. You'll want their airy grace as contrast in your garden and in bouquets.

Plants last only 5 to 6 weeks in the summer, but you'll probably want them in the garden far longer than that. The trick to keeping a good supply of the plants is to sow the seeds about every 3 or 4 weeks instead of just once at the beginning of the season.

Scatter the seeds in drifts in open sunny spaces, in front of shrubs, or over old bulb beds. Rake soil over lightly to cover and firm in the seeds by pressing them down with a board or simply by walking over the area.

Varieties: 'Covent Garden,' white, is widely used. A pink variety is available from some seed firms.

Bachelor's Button

Centaurea cyanus (Cornflower). Photo on page 29.

Perky, rayed blossoms of bachelor's button, in flag-blue, pink, rose, or white, will give you pleasure all spring with abundant flowers for the garden and for cutting. Tall varieties grow upright to 2½ feet and have good stems for arrangements. Rather unkempt in appearance, the lanky stems and shaggy gray-green foliage looks best behind an edging such as candytuft or sweet alyssum. Dwarf types, 12 to 15 inches high, are more compact.

Bachelor's button is simple to grow; seeds are large, easy to plant, and sprout quickly. Start the seeds outdoors in full sun where the plants are to grow; seedlings do not transplant well. Plants do best in light, neutral soil. Since bachelor's button blooms only until July and then burns out, the earlier the seeds are started, the better. Except where temperatures drop to 15 or 20°, bachelor's button should be seeded in late summer or fall. Where winters are severe, plant seeds outdoors when soil is dry enough to work.

Flowers come in single and mixed colors. 'Tall Blue' is a favorite variety for gardeners wanting tall stems and blue flowers. 'Jubilee Gem' is a dwarf variety with blue flowers. 'Polka Dot' is a dwarf with mixed colors.

Balsam

See *Impatiens.*

Bells of Ireland

Molucella laevis (Shellflower). Photo on page 29.

Tiny, aromatic, white flowers on this plant are surrounded by enlarged bell or shell-shaped calyxes that look like big green flowers. Plants grow 1½ to 3 feet tall; their graceful curving stems have blooms along their entire length. As cut flowers (the leaves are usually removed, as they were from the plants in the photograph on page 29.), bells of Ireland are handsome and long lasting. When dried, the flowers turn creamy gold.

Bells of Ireland seeds are somewhat erratic in germination. If you live in a short-summer climate, try starting the seeds in flats indoors as suggested for butterfly flower (page 30). Otherwise, sow the seeds outdoors in a sunny location and warm soil in the early summer for fall flowers (or in August if the warm season is extremely long). It is important to keep the seeds warm during the germination period. Regular applications of plant food and ample water will give you full, extra-long flower stalks.

To dry the flower spikes for winter bouquets, cut them when they're in full bloom. Remove the leaves and tie the spikes in clusters; then hang them upside down in a cool, well-ventilated place to dry.

ANAGALLIS

BABY-BLUE-EYES

ANCHUSA CAPENSIS

ASTER

BELLS OF IRELAND

BABY'S BREATH

BACHELOR'S BUTTON

Black-Eyed Susan Vine

Thunbergia alata (Clockvine). Photo on page 31.

This dainty twining vine has attractive 1½-inch-wide tubular flowers in cream, orange, yellow, and white with purple-black throats. Though a perennial, it grows fast enough to bloom the first year and can be treated as an annual. In sheltered locations and mild-winter areas, plants may live over to the following season.

Black-eyed Susan vine is easiest to grow in hanging containers where its neat, short runners can cascade over the sides; it can also be trained on low trellises.

The vines grow rapidly with warmth and moisture, so plant seeds outdoors in warm soil and in a sunny location. If you grow them in containers, feed about once a month.

Blue Lace Flower

Trachymene caerulea, formerly *Didiscus caerulea*. Photo on page 31.

A late spring bloomer, blue lace flower is at its best as a cut flower. Two to three-inch-wide umbrellalike clusters of tiny flowers grow on 1 to 2-foot branching plants that have finely divided leaves.

Blue lace flower looks very much like the prairie wildflower Queen Anne's lace. It is grown mostly for flowers, since its growth form is too open and uneven to make it a good bedding plant. Unfortunately, the flowers stay open only for a few weeks during the late spring. You may want to make successive plantings to keep up their supply. Plant seeds in full sun outdoors in the spring when the soil is warm and dry. Seedlings seem to resent transplanting.

While blue is the best-known color, you can get white and pink varieties from specialty seed outlets.

Browallia

Browallia species (Amethyst flower). Photo on page 31.

Browallia is an unusually versatile flower: it blooms all summer in warm, shaded beds, pots, or hanging containers and will continue blooming through the winter if brought indoors as a house plant. Attractive in arrangements, the flowers come in blue, violet, or white, the blue blossoms having white throats.

You have a choice of two species. *B. americana,* a branching plant, 1 to 2 feet high, has lopsided clusters of lobelialike, ½-inch blooms. *B. speciosa* is sprawling in growth and 2 to 3 feet tall with petunialike blossoms 1½ to 2 inches across. Dwarf varieties of *B. speciosa* are rather bushy and 12 to 15 inches tall, they come in separate colors: Blue Bells Improved, a strain with lavender-blue flowers, and 'Silver Bells,' a snow-white variety, are favorites.

Sow seeds in flats indoors 8 to 10 weeks prior to warm weather. At 70 to 75°, seeds should sprout in 2 weeks. Seedlings transplant easily, but don't set them out until all shade trees are in full leaf. Give plants plenty of fertilizer and water, particularly during hot weather, and make sure they receive afternoon shade.

Butterfly Flower

Schizanthus pinnatus (Poor man's orchid). Photo on page 31.

Butterfly flower (or schizanthus) is popular in mild-climate areas of California for winter and early spring bloom. Sensitive to both heat and frost, it also does well in mountain sections and in northern areas where summer nights are cool. The 1½-foot-high plants have lacy foliage nearly hidden under tumbling masses of colorful, 1-inch-wide flowers. Blossoms resemble small orchids in lilac, soft pink, purple, rose, and white with vari-colored markings. The flowers do well under the shade of trees and in containers.

In mild-winter areas, start seeds in August for winter bloom. Seeds are maddeningly slow to germinate. Since they can take up to 4 months to sprout, you may find it less trouble to buy small plants from the nursery. To speed up the germination of seeds, fill a plastic dish with vermiculite or sphagnum moss, moisten, drain off excess water, and scatter seeds. Cover the seeds with 1/16 inch of the planting material and place the container in a plastic bag. Put it on a window sill and water lightly once a week. When the first seedlings emerge, remove the bag. In 6 or 8 weeks, the little plants will be ready to set out. After transplanting, protect the seedlings for 2 or 3 days from the sun and wind with newspaper hoods or with a lath shelter.

Outdoors in the garden, start seeds in a shaded bed with good soil, as rich in humus as soil for tuberous begonias. Scatter a few seeds, cover lightly, and keep the soil moist. Transplant when seedlings have 4 to 6 leaves.

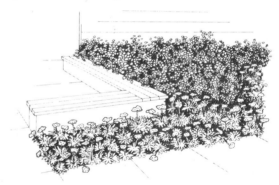

BUTTERFLY FLOWER and fairy primrose are two cool-season annuals for spring or fall color combinations.

Butterfly flower combines well with fairy primrose and cineraria, sharing the same cultural requirements with them: light shade and moist, well-drained soil. The cut flowers last 3 to 4 days.

Calendula

Calendula officinalis (Pot marigold). Photo on page 33.

In golden shades from apricot to yellow, calendula's big-rayed flowers are from 2½ to 4½ inches across. Because they somewhat resemble marigolds and the leaves were once

BROWALLIA

BLACK-EYED SUSAN VINE

BLUE LACE FLOWER

BUTTERFLY FLOWER

31

cooked as a vegetable, they bear the nickname "pot marigold." A cool-season annual, calendula will provide spring or fall color and, in mild areas, can be an outstanding feature of winter gardens.

Calendula is a bushy plant with long, narrow, slightly sticky leaves. Regular varieties grow 1½ to 3 feet tall in warm weather and a bit shorter in cooler climates. Dwarf types grow to 12 inches high. On both regular and dwarf varieties, the single, double, or semi-double flowers are usually borne one to a stem. Flower colors run the gamut from cream and pale yellow to apricot, gold, orange, and persimmon. Yellows and oranges are frequent favorites.

Sow calendula seeds in flats or in the garden. In mild climates, plant seeds in July or August for bloom by Christmas and in September or October for spring bloom. Where winters are cold, either start seeds indoors in winter and plant out very carefully in the spring or sow seeds early in the summer for color in late summer or fall. Seeds usually take about a week to germinate. Most nurseries sell calendulas in flats as bedding plants.

For earliest color, place seeds or plants in full sun. In hot desert areas, however, plant in light shade. When seedlings are well on their way, thin to about 12 inches apart.

Calendulas tolerate poor soil but require good drainage and benefit from occasional cultivation. Water regularly to keep the soil slightly damp, being careful to avoid soaking. To encourage branching and to produce the most flowers, pinch back the main stem when the first flower head starts to form.

Snails and slugs relish calendula's fresh fall foliage, so plan on setting out meal or pellet bait. Occasional infestations of cabbage worms or aphids can be controlled with a multipurpose insecticide.

For cut flowers, pick blooms in bud or near-bud; open blossoms wilt very rapidly. Calendulas are effective when displayed with substantial green foliage and combine well with blue bachelor's buttons.

The Pacific Beauty class, bred for heat tolerance, contains clear colors: 'Flame' and 'Persimmon' are excellent choices. You can buy single colors or mixtures.

California Poppy

Eschscholzia californica. Photo on page 33.

Few flowers ask less and give more than California poppies. Their only requirement is light, well-drained soil. Just toss a handful of seeds on the ground and let the rain wash them in. You'll be rewarded with lacy, blue-green foliage and satiny, cup-shaped, long-stemmed flowers in bright profusion from spring through late summer on 1 to 2-foot-tall plants.

California poppy, the state flower of California where it blooms freely in fields and hills, is not a true poppy (see poppy, page 54). It is a perennial usually grown in gardens as an annual.

In the wild, California poppy is a single flower in glowing orange-gold. Seedsmen have developed a mixture called Mission Bells that contains striking double or semi-double flowers in cream, deep red, scarlet, pink, orange, and yellow. Blossoms close up each night like furled umbrellas, opening again in the morning.

Naturalize California poppies in dry spots along drives, in hard-to-cultivate areas, or anywhere that a spot of cheerful spring or summer color is needed.

Sow seeds in the fall or early spring, pulling the plants out when their foliage yellows or leaving them to come back next year. Plants reseed themselves readily, and, unless you are diligent about removing the long thin seedpods, you may find your garden full of more plants than desired.

Blooms make good cut flowers and will last longest if you pick them as buds and place immediately in cold water.

Calliopsis

Coreopsis tinctoria. Photo on page 33.

A summer blooming relative of the sunflower, calliopsis is one of the easiest annuals to grow. Tall varieties reach 3 feet high and are best used as background plants because of their loose, open growth habit. Dwarf calliopsis grows 8 to 12 inches high and makes an unusual edging.

Calliopsis has daisylike flowers growing at the ends of long, wiry stems. Some have golden yellow rays that may be slightly reddish brown at the base and brownish purple in the center. Others are almost solid brown or mahogany.

Sow seeds outdoors where plants are to remain. Cold temperatures won't harm the seeds, so you can plant them in the spring as soon as the soil can be worked. Calliopsis blooms all summer long, except for the low-growing types which burn out in the late summer.

Candytuft

Iberis species. Photo on page 33.

Fragrance would be reason enough to grow this versatile, free-blooming, and lovely flower. There are several perennial types but two main annual species of *Iberis:* hyacinth-flowered candytuft (*I. amara*) and globe candytuft (*I. umbellata*).

Hyacinth-flowered candytuft (*I. amara*), sometimes called rocket candytuft, carries snowy white flowers in 10 to 15-inch hyacinthlike spikes, 3 or more to each plant. It blooms in early spring, along with daffodils, tulips, and other bulbs, and makes an excellent cut flower.

Hyacinth-flowered candytuft is rarely grown outside mild-winter areas, where it is almost always planted in the fall. The early-blooming plants are intolerant of high heat.

Globe candytuft (*I. umbellata*) grows in 12 to 15-inch-high mounds. Dwarf hybrids reach 6 inches tall. In late spring and early summer, globe candytuft is covered with lilac, pink, rose, salmon, or white flowers growing in tight rounded clusters. For spectacular drifts of pastel flowers, plant candytuft in extensive borders or use it as an edging. Enjoy the blooms in fresh bouquets.

Sow seeds of globe candytuft in late fall or early spring. Since plants are somewhat difficult to transplant, it is best to broadcast seed where you want it to grow.

Canterbury Bells

Campanula medium. Photo on page 35.

Canterbury bells is a sturdy, free-flowering biennial that can be treated as an annual. Like most biennials, it blooms

CALENDULA

CALIFORNIA POPPY

GLOBE CANDYTUFT

CALLIOPSIS

33

in the second year after you plant the seeds. Buy nursery plants if you want blooms immediately.

Plants grow 2½ to 4 feet tall and have strong, heavily flowered stems that are excellent for cutting. Single or double flowers, shaped like bells or urns, come in shades of lavender, pink, rose, violet, and white. The toothed leaves are 3 to 5 inches long on the upper stems and 6 to 10 inches long down towards the base. Though biennial, a double-flowered form, 'Calycanthema,' (commonly called cup-and-saucer) is popular. Canterbury bells is available in single and mixed colors.

Sow seeds in late spring for plants that will bloom the following spring. If you buy nursery plants, set them 15 to 18 inches apart in the garden. Plant in good garden soil and in full sun. In very warm climates, plant in partial shade. Water thoroughly during the growing and blooming season. Canterbury bells often reseeds itself.

Cardinal Climber

Quamoclit sloteri. Photo on page 35.

This twining, free-flowering vine, growing to 20 feet high, is useful as a quick, temporary screen. The dark green leaves are deeply cut and resemble the foliage of some ferns; the flowers are like deep-throated morning glories, 1½ to 2 inches long and red with white centers. Blossoms remain open except during the hottest part of the day.

Plant seeds in full sun where plants are to remain and will have room to climb from 10 to 20 feet. Train them on strings leading up to the eaves on a sunny side of the house where their light, airy foliage will shade without cutting off the view.

Celosia

Celosia argentea (Cockscomb). Photos on page 35.

If you dare, plant celosia. It has such striking color that it immediately attracts attention. Use celosia correctly and you'll have a garden of breathtaking brilliance. But use it haphazardly and celosia will turn your garden into a confusion of clashing colors. Celosia grows from 6 inches to 3 feet tall, depending on the type. Two kinds are available: plume celosia and true cockscomb.

If you'd like bright background flowers, use the plume celosia (*C. a.* 'Plumosa'). It is a large plant with many feathery flower clusters growing in plumes resembling a horse's tail. Lovely dwarf forms make spectacular edgings. 'Forest Fire' is a striking bedding or background plant with bright scarlet plumes and bronze-red foliage. It is good with white petunias in the foreground. 'Golden Triumph' is golden yellow in color, grading into deep golds.

The true or crested cockscombs (*C. a.* 'Cristata') have velvety flowers arranged in big folded or fan-shaped clusters. The newer types are 1½ to 2 feet high and best massed in beds. Dwarf forms grow only 6 to 8 inches tall. 'Fireglow,' (All-America) is 20 to 24 inches high, with huge, deep rich red, velvety flower clusters. 'Jewel Box' is a 4 to 6-inch dwarf.

Gentle colors are available (pink, rose, and wine-red), but if you want something wilder, try the vivid reds, scarlet, and gold. Watch also for striking foliage color—maroon or dark green is easier to use in the garden than the chartreuse-green and some of the other bright colors.

Since celosia is available at nurseries as bedding plants and seeds sprout and grow rapidly, you'll find little need to start seeds indoors in the winter except where summers are extremely short. Seeds should not be planted outdoors until the soil is warm. Plants grow rapidly in full sun, the hotter the better. Celosia won't tolerate shade.

Flower arrangers dry celosia for winter bouquets. It is one of the few flowers that holds its true color when dried. Fresh plumes of celosia combine effectively with chrysanthemums, gladiolus, marigolds, or zinnias.

Chinese Forget-Me-Not

Cynoglossum amabile. Photo on page 38.

If you have cool summers, you'll enjoy the sweet scent and rich blue of these dainty clustered flowers. Larger than cape forget-me-not *(Anchusa capensis),* the tiny blossoms and gray-green foliage grow on plants that are 1½ to 2 feet tall. In the garden, Chinese forget-me-not combines well with wildflowers, candytuft, or impatiens. Unfortunately, the flowers wilt quickly after cutting.

Sow seeds outdoors where plants are to remain. Seeds are not harmed by scattering on cold soil in very early spring, and if you do sow in early spring, plants will have a head start on the blooming season. Give them sun and regular watering, and you'll be rewarded with flowers from late spring through summer.

Cineraria

Senecio cruentus. Photo on page 38.

In the cool shade where cinerarias thrive, their daisylike flowers sparkle in light to dark shades of blue, magenta, pink, purple, and shining white during the spring months in California gardens—especially along the coast. And in these areas cineraria often remains the perennial it is. In warmer locations it is usually grown as an annual and replaced each year with fresh new plants.

Potted cineraria is often sold in full bloom at nurseries —and most gardeners buy their plants. The large-flowered strains, with blossoms in big, compact clusters and mixed colors, are the most popular. These plants grow 12 to 15 inches high and have large, attractive, heartshaped leaves. Once established in the garden, cineraria often self sows.

Cinerarias are fairly easy to grow from seed sown in the late fall in mild-winter areas. Transplant seedlings when they are quite small and they will come into bloom quicker than if you wait until they are larger.

For best results, grow cinerarias in shaded areas in cool, moist, leafy, well-drained soil; poorly drained soil causes root rot. Water them lavishly during their growing period; on warm days you may have to sprinkle them several times or they will wilt. Plants grown in containers require frequent feeding—usually every 2 weeks.

Leaf miner is cineraria's worst pest. Larvae tunnel through the leaves and make plants look unsightly. Once

CELOSIA 'PLUMOSA'

CANTERBURY BELLS

CARDINAL CLIMBER

CELOSIA 'CRISTATA'

the miner gets inside the leaf, it's difficult to control, but early preventive spraying with malathion at 15-day intervals usually keeps it away. The same sprays control aphids, whiteflies, and other pests. You'll also need to bait for slugs and snails.

Cinerarias combine beautifully with such other shade-loving plants as ferns and fibrous begonias. They are excellent in pots for color in shady outdoor living areas.

Clarkia

Clarkia species. Photos on page 38.

Clarkia *(C. unguiculata* or *C. elegans)* and godetia *(C. amoena)* are showy Western wildflowers that thrive in light soil in cool summer climates, where they put on a wonderful display of flowers from late spring to fall. They rarely do well where summers are humid and temperatures average above 80°.

Clarkia has reddish stalks that grow from 1 to 4 feet tall with small narrow leaves and 1½ to 2-inch flowers on alternate sides from base to tip. Buds lower down on the branches bloom first and will sometimes form seed pods before the top buds even open. The total effect is spiky.

In the wild, clarkia usually has single flowers, cup-shaped and slightly flaring, with petals resembling colored tissue paper in lavender, rose, and white. Seedsmen have developed spendid double flowers in mixtures that include the colors above along with crimson, orange, pink, salmon, and creamy yellow.

Godetia grows 1 to 2½ feet tall in mounds that are covered with upright buds that open into cup-shaped single or double flowers, about 2 inches across. The flowers are usually bicolored with red or white streaks on pink, rose, or salmon.

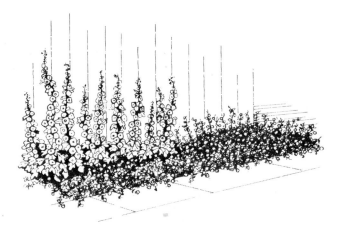

CLARKIA'S upright stems and mounding growth are a perfect filler for hollyhocks accented against a fence.

Like most wildflowers, clarkia and godetia require little care when planted in a suitable location and climate. Since they don't transplant well, sow the seeds where plants are to grow in the early spring or—in mild-winter areas—during the fall. Scatter the seeds so plants will grow in clumps.

Try clarkia and godetia with taller flowers, such as foxglove or hollyhock, and in fresh arrangements. After seeds sprout, water sparingly.

Cleome

Cleome spinosa (Spider flower). Photo on page 40.

Large and shrublike, cleome makes an attractive hedge and is one of the few annuals that is easy to grow in all 50 states. Its open, fluffy flower clusters, 1 to 2 feet long, bloom through the summer and into fall; its divided foliage gives it an airy look. Flowers come in pink, rose, or white, with extremely long stamens and long thin seed pods that form below the blooms. (Hence the name spider flower.) Cleome needs plenty of room to grow: in warm areas, plants reach 6 feet high and spread to 4 or 5 feet wide.

Use cleome for backgrounds or in large patio tubs. It is very attractive against grapestake fences or solid walls; reflected heat doesn't harm it. You can use the flower clusters and dried seed pods in large arrangements with such other substantial blooms as gladiolus and zinnias.

Seeds sprout readily in warm soil outdoors, and plants grow rapidly in full sun. Only where summers are quite short is it necessary to start seeds indoors. Keep cleome on the dry side or it will become rank.

Coleus

Coleus blumei. Photo on page 40.

Colorful is too mild a description for coleus. A perennial usually grown as a bedding annual in cold-winter climates, coleus—prized for its vivid and brilliant leaves—is also a popular house plant. The large toothed, oval leaves (brown, chartreuse, fluorescent red, magenta, maroon, orange, and purple) come in both single and variegated colors. Plants grow 2 to 3 feet high in the garden. Try them outdoors in lightly shaded borders or in containers and bring cuttings indoors to grow in pots during winter.

The spikes of white or dark blue flowers can be pinched back to keep plants growing vigorously. It is a good idea to pinch out the growing tips of the plants regularly to encourage branching.

Grow coleus from seeds or cuttings. With seeds, you will get best results planting them indoors in flats. For quick germination, seeds require bottom heat of 70 to 75°. Transplant to warm, rich, well-drained soil receiving strong, indirect light or moderate shade for best colors. Provide ample water and feed regularly with high nitrogen fertilizer. No two plants will be alike.

The simplest way to perpetuate your favorite varieties of coleus is by rooting cuttings. Simply snap off side shoots from an established plant, remove all but the tip leaves, and place the shoots in a glass of water. When roots are ½ inch long, pot each shoot individually in a mixture of soil, sand, and peat moss or leaf mold. Aphids and mealybugs enjoy coleus—control with malathion.

Use coleus in arrangements as a background or filler; plain-leafed varieties are less likely to overwhelm your other flowers. Place the stems in deep, cold water to stiffen them before arranging.

Cosmos

Cosmos species. Photo on page 40.

Daisylike cosmos blossoms are borne on long, pliant, deceptively fragile-looking, 2 to 6-foot stems. But the wind blows right through the fine foliage without breaking the plants, and their bobbing in any breeze adds motion to your garden.

The common cosmos (*C. bippinatus*) comes in single flowers 2 to 3 inches across in shades of magenta, pink, white, and lavender with tufted yellow centers. Another species, *C. sulphureus,* has semidouble and double flowers in gold and vermilion, some with striped petals.

Sow seeds in full sun and soil that is not overrich, any time from early spring through midsummer. For earliest bloom, sow in flats during late winter and transplant later. Tall cosmos look best as background plants or in groups among tall shrubs.

Cut freshly opened cosmos blossoms for bouquets; plunge them immediately into cool water to keep flowers and foliage from wilting. Arrange in loose, airy masses, using plenty of foliage. You can find seeds in single colors and mixes.

Dahlia, bedding

Dahlia merckii (Dwarf dahlia). Photo on page 41.

Though perennial, bedding dahlias are usually handled as annuals. If you start them from seeds, they'll produce flowers the same year, along with seeds and tubers that you can use to propagate new plants with next year. The compact plants grow from 15 to 24 inches high and have double, semi-double, or single 2 to 3-inch flowers in abundance all summer. Clear, luminous flower colors range from pastels to deep rich reds and purples.

Start seeds indoors in cold areas; they sprout rapidly after the weather warms and require only 6 to 8 weeks to grow to planting out size. Seedlings transplant very well. In warmer regions, sow seeds directly in open ground. You can usually find bedding dahlias at nurseries in flats or in single pots. Be sure to place plants in rich, well-drained soil in full sun. In very hot areas, provide light afternoon shade. Water frequently.

Dahlia's flowers are striking in arrangements, and cutting the blossoms prolongs the plant's blooming season. If you cut the flowers just before they are fully open, they'll last at least 4 or 5 days.

Among the many strains, Early Bird Mixed blooms soonest; Unwin's Dwarf Mix has semidouble flowers in a wide range of colors on 24-inch plants; and Fall Festival has bronze-red foliage and apricot, crimson, purple, scarlet, and yellow flowers.

Dianthus

Dianthus species. Photo on page 41.

Of the many dianthus species, those most often grown in annual flower gardens are pinks (*D. chinensis* and *D. plumarius*), sweet William (*D. barbatus*), and carnation (*D. caryophyllus*). They all share the spare, gray-green foliage, clovelike scent, and pinked edge petals typical of dianthus.

Pinks generally bloom in the late spring or early summer and bear loose clusters of several pink, red, rose, or white blossoms on foot-long stems. Annual types grow quickly from seeds sown outdoors in the fall or early spring in full sun. Plants tolerate almost any climate except extreme heat, and since they are frost resistant, pinks serve as a winter annual in areas where summers are very hot. Among the varieties you'll find both single-flowered and carnation-flowered types in single and mixed colors.

Sweet William (*D. barbatus*) is a 1 to 2-foot plant; regular and dwarf biennial and annual flowering varieties are available. 'Red Monarch,' bright red and 10 inches tall, and 'Wee Willie,' 3 to 4 inches tall, are popular annual flowering varieties. The dwarf types make fine edging plants.

Carnations (*D. caryophyllus*) fall into two distinct classifications: florist carnations and border carnations. Both have double flowers, bluish green leaves, and branching leafy stems, often becoming woody at the base. Flower colors for both range from maroon through red and pink to salmon and yellow to cream and white, with some bicolors.

Florist carnations have flowers 3 inches across borne on wiry stems 16 to 24 inches tall. Be sure to stake the stems or they'll grow tall and straight until the buds nearly open and then fall over from the weight.

Border carnations are bushier and more compact than florist carnations and grow 12 to 14 inches high. Flowers are slightly smaller than the florist type and bloom in profusion.

Carnations are perennials treated as annuals except in mild winter climates, but if the seeds are sown very early in the spring, plants will bloom in late summer or early fall. Plants like full sun and light, fast-draining soil that is neutral or slightly alkaline. Cutting the flowers will prolong the blooming period.

Among the many carnation types available in seed packets or as nursery plants are Chabaud's Giant Improved strain (florist carnations in single or mixed colors) and the Dwarf Fragrance Mix, a border carnation in mixed colors.

Fairy Primrose

Primula malacoides. Photo on page 41.

In cool, moist climates where frosts are rare, fairy primrose is a delight for winter and early spring bloom. A lacy and delicate annual form of the perennial primrose, fairy primrose bears loose, lacy whorls of lavender, pink, rose, carmine-red, or white blossoms on slender, 1-foot-high stems above a rosette of round green leaves. Planted in the shade of high-branching trees, with spring bulbs, or in containers, the flowers will bloom for weeks.

Many nurseries sell fairy primrose in flats or pots. To grow plants from seed takes some initial effort, but these flowers are worth it. In August sow seeds along shallow furrows in flats of soil covered with ½ inch of vermiculite or sand. Cover the seeds not more than ⅛ inch deep. Set the flats in water until they can absorb no more moisture, then cover with plastic sheeting and place in a shady location. Water once a week from the bottom until seeds sprout before removing the plastic. When seedlings have four leaves, transplant them into shaded beds that have been enriched with a 1-inch layer of peat moss or leaf mold.

(Continued on page 39)

CHINESE FORGET-ME-NOT

CINERARIA

CLARKIA ELEGANS

GODETIA

38

(Continued from page 37)

Be sure to keep the soil moist and to protect the plants from drying winds.

Fairy primrose adds an airy grace to arrangements of flowers such as cyclamen, freesias, daffodils, and tulips.

Four O'clock

Mirabilis jalapa. Photo on page 41.

When it comes to blooming, four o'clocks are truly late sleepers. Not only do they wait until midsummer to bloom, but as their common name suggests, they keep their flowers shut tight until late afternoon unless the day is cloudy. Nevertheless, the plants' dense, dark green foliage and profusion of trumpet-shaped, lavender, pink, salmon, white, and yellow flowers act as refreshers in flower gardens that may be past their prime in fall. And they continue to bloom until frost blackens the foliage.

Actually, four o'clocks are perennials in mild-winter areas, but they are grown as annuals where winters are cold. Plants grow to 3 or 4 feet high in one summer and spread to 3 feet. They make excellent temporary low hedges or screens and will quickly fill in tight, little-used areas.

Four o'clocks are especially popular in urban communities because they are little affected by excess dust, fumes, and soot—simply wash them off with an occasional sprinkling.

Plants grow rapidly from the large seeds scattered in open, sunny, warm soil after frosts. Once you start four o'clocks, you're apt to find them coming up every summer, even if you shear them to the ground when they are through blooming in the fall.

Foxglove

Digitalis purpurea. Photo on page 43.

Although it is biennial, this species of foxglove will often bloom in the first year. Characterized by large woolly leaves that unfold in handsome rosettes, this bold plant sends up 2½ to 8-foot spikes of nodding, tubular flowers shaped like the fingers of a glove in pink, purple, rose, white, or yellow. The flowers are dotted with darker colors on the inside. Larger types deserve big gardens; one strain called Dwarf Foxy Mixed grows to 2½ to 3 feet tall and will bloom the first year.

To be sure of getting bloom the first year, start seeds indoors in early spring. Transplant seedlings into small pots from which they may be set out in your garden. Where winters are severe but there is no protective snow cover, mulch plants in late winter to keep frost from heaving them out of the ground. Flowers will bloom from May to September.

Plant foxglove in full or partial shade and in rich moist soil where there is protection from wind. After the first flowering, cut the main spike; side shoots will develop and bloom. Plants reseed with great ease.

You'll find two main strains of large foxgloves: Excelsior Hybrids have large pink, purple, rose, white, and primrose-yellow flowers arranged closely in a horizontal position all around the stem; Shirley Hybrids have large, bell-shaped blooms in shades of soft pink to deep rose, spotted with brown, crimson, or maroon.

Gaillardia

Gaillardia pulchella (Annual gaillardia).
Photo on page 43.

A Texas native, gaillardia thrives in sun and heat. Easy to grow, it has 2-inch-wide flowers in bright hot shades of bronze, gold, red, and yellow borne on 10-inch to 2-foot-long whiplike stems. Foliage is toothed and succulent. Stems of taller types may need staking.

Plant seeds in warm, well-drained soil in full sun after the last frost to enjoy blooms all summer. Gaillardia is an interesting cut flower that will keep for several days.

A variety called 'Picta,' with large flower heads, is the usual garden form. The Lollipop series is a compact dwarf with fully double ball-shaped flowerheads. The Double Gaiety strain has claret, rose, yellow, orange, and maroon colors which often appear on the same flower. Double Lorenziana has globular flower heads in a wide range of colors from white to red and often variegated.

Globe Amaranth

Gomphrena globosa. Photo on page 43.

Bushy, branching plants growing 2 or 3 feet high, globe amaranth is covered with rounded, cloverlike flower heads ¾ inch wide. Colors are magenta, purple, violet, or white. Flower heads have a papery quality that classes them as "everlasting." Globe amaranth is an excellent plant for hot-summer climates.

In hot climates, plant seeds (covered with a cottony lint) outdoors in warm soil as you would zinnias. Globe amaranth will grow well in cool northern states, but the seeds should be started indoors 8 to 10 weeks prior to the frost-free date.

The fresh-cut blossoms are an interesting addition to mixed bouquets. Flowers dry quickly and easily, retaining their color and shape for winter arrangements.

Godelia

See *Clarkia.*

Hollyhock

Althaea rosea. Photo on page 43.

A robust country perennial, hollyhock also makes an appearance in surprisingly elegant annual versions ranging in height from 6 feet down to a 24-inch dwarf that will suit even the smallest garden. You can find single, double, and fringed flowers in subtle single shades and glorious mixtures that include cream, pink, red, rose, scarlet, and white. Read the seed packets carefully to be sure you are getting an annual type guaranteed to bloom the same year you plant them. Three of the most interesting types are the compact 'Silver Puffs,' a delicate, silvery pink double flower on bushy plants only 2 feet tall; Summer Carnival Mixed, having 5 to 6-foot-high spikes with double flowers

COSMOS

CLEOME

COLEUS

DIANTHUS

FAIRY PRIMROSE

BEDDING DAHLIA

FOUR O'CLOCK

in a mixture of every hollyhock color; and Madcap Annual Mixed, a popular annual hollyhock strain in mixed and bicolors.

Start seeds in peat pots indoors in very early spring; transplant seedlings outdoors into moist rich soil when the danger of frost is past. Plants may reseed themselves.

Rust, a disease common to hollyhocks, can be controlled by removing and destroying the first leaves on which it appears or by dusting with sulphur.

If you have a young child in your family, show him how to make hollyhock dolls. Snap off a flower so that a ¾-inch stem remains. Pluck one fat bud for a head, force it onto the stem, and presto!—you have a doll with a fancy skirt.

Impatiens

Impatiens species. Photos on page 46.

Attractive, sturdy, and easy to grow, impatiens will adorn your garden through the summer, amuse you with their unusual seed capsules in the fall, and provide indoor color during the winter. Two species are most frequently grown: *I. balsamina* and *I. walleriana*.

Balsam (*I. balsamina*), a sturdy, bushy plant growing 8 inches to 2 feet tall (depending on variety) is covered all summer long with long-lasting blooms that look like azaleas or miniature camellias.

The flowers, single or double, are borne on leafy stems. Colors range from white and pink through purple with some mixed and bi-colored types that are very popular. Dwarf varieties are fine as edgings and make excellent container plants.

This plant's fat seeds sprout in 4 to 5 days when planted in warm, moist soil outdoors. You can also start seeds indoors and set out transplants later. Give them plenty of water and feed about once a month; otherwise the plants will lose their glossy dark green color.

Balsam requires a warm, sunny location; it won't tolerate wet or cold weather. If your summers are very hot and long, however, select a location where plants will be protected from afternoon sun.

Balsam is not a good cut flower. Its nickname touch-me-not comes from its seed pods which spring open when tapped sharply and fling seeds far and wide.

Attractive, obliging, and easy to grow, impatiens (*I. walleriana*, formerly called *I. holstii* or *I. sultanii*) will adorn your garden all summer. Flat, starry, half-dollar-sized flowers in clear red, pink, white, lavender, purple, or orange rise above glossy dark green leaves, blooming from spring through frost in half-shade or shade. The handsome plants go equally well in beds, pots, tubs, and hanging containers, growing in mounds slightly wider than they are tall. Plants range in height from 6 to 24 inches. Impatiens has the rare virtue of appealing only to people: bugs, snails, fungi, and viruses avoid it.

In the fall, impatiens forms seed capsules similar to those of balsam, which explode when tapped sharply. Before the first frost, choose a couple of plants to dig up and bring indoors in pots for winter bloom.

You can buy impatiens in flats or pots from the nursery or start seeds indoors 10 to 12 weeks before warm weather. Use bottom heat provided by a heating cable (70 to 75°). Set 2 or 3 plants out in a large pot or arrange them in groups under trees. Impatiens appreciates fair to good soil

and frequent watering. Don't feed them unless you want more leaves and fewer flowers. Blooms do not make good cut flowers.

Among the types of *I. walleriana* you'll want to investigate are the Elfin Dwarf series, 8 to 10 inches tall in separate and mixed colors; the Dwarf Imp strain, 12 to 14 inches tall in both single and mixed colors; and taller kinds, such as the Holstii Mixture which reaches 20 inches. Some bicolor varieties may also appeal to you.

Kochia

Kochia scoparia, sold as *K. 'Childsii'*
(Summer cypress, Belvedere). Photo on page 46.

These are foliage plants, usually grown close together as screens or individually for their gently rounded, 3-foot-high columnar form. Branches are densely clothed with soft, very narrow leaves, making the plants too thick to see through. Their green color is pleasant; their billowy form makes up for the lack of flower color.

Seed kochia in full sun outdoors. It grows quickly and can be shaped by pruning to create a formal hedge. Owners of new homes often use kochia for temporary shrubs until the weather is cool enough to set out woody plants. Kochia tolerates high heat, yet will perform well in short-summer areas.

One variety, called Mexican fire bush (*K. s. 'Trichophylla,'* as well as *K. 'Childsii'*), turns red with the first frost.

Larkspur

Delphinium ajacis. Photo on page 46.

The annual version of perennial delphinium, larkspur will give a strong vertical accent to your garden in late spring and early summer. The tall full spikes of clustered, 1 to 1½-inch spurred flowers come in rich blues, as well as a variety of rosy shades and white. Easy to grow, the plants range in height from 1 to 4 feet. Smaller types look dashing in containers; larger kinds make excellent background plants. You will want a solid edging, perhaps of godetias or candytuft, in front of larkspur to conceal the low foliage, which browns and mildews in early summer. Tallest larkspur varieties may need staking.

Plant seeds in late summer where winters are mild; where winters are severe, sow seeds in very early spring, no later than mid-April. Scatter seeds over roughly prepared beds of rich soil, watering thoroughly. The washing action will cover seeds sufficiently. Seedlings are quite hardy and can be transplanted successfully when small. Water frequently and feed occasionally.

Larkspur is a valuable cut flower that looks equally good in masses of single colors or in harmonizing shades. Blooms will keep for 3 or 4 days. Try drying some branches of larkspur for winter bouquets.

Look for two main types: the base-branching plants, in the Regal and Imperial classes; and the hyacinth-flowered group, which has a single non-branching stalk. Both can be found in single or mixed colors.

GLOBE AMARANTH

HOLLYHOCK

GAILLARDIA

FOXGLOVE

Linaria

Linaria maroccana (Baby snapdragon).
Photo on page 48.

Tiny, dainty, fast-blooming linaria resembles miniature snapdragons, having two-toned flowers in shades of lavender, maroon, red, white, and yellow. In cool-summer areas, it blooms from May to September; in warm areas it burns out by July. The colors are soft and the stems and leaves are very fine, so you'll want to plant linaria in extensive drifts to show them up properly. Use linaria to add color to the fading foliage in tulip or daffodil beds, to brighten meadows or lanes, or to fill in among chrysanthemums while they are growing and setting buds.

Sow linaria seeds in full sun during fall or very early spring. Fairy Bouquet, 8 to 10 inches high, has pastel flowers in mixed shades; Northern Lights is taller, growing to 15 inches, and produces smaller flowers in deep tones.

Lobelia

Lobelia erinus. Photo on page 48.

Offering a Gainsborough palette of rich blues, lobelia grows in low mounds that bloom from May to October. You can find lobelia in white and violet-rose, but it is the blues you will remember: baby blue, sky blue, electric blue, sapphire blue. With leaves that echo flower color so closely that they add to its intensity, lobelia is an ideal border plant. It can also adorn rock gardens and containers, and a trailing form is perfect for hanging baskets.

Plants are small and neat, 4 to 8 inches high and slightly wider than they are tall, covered with blossoms interspersed with thin leaves that are bluish on blue plants and red-streaked on red plants. They will bloom all summer and well into fall if you shear them back after the first main blooming period. In cool climates, you can place them in full sun; warmer regions, partial shade or light shade will keep them in bloom during hot weather.

If you live in an area where spring comes early, you may sow seed directly outdoors. But since lobelia is slow to reach maturity from seed, you might prefer to buy young plants from the nursery or to start the seeds indoors in the winter in a greenhouse or coldframe. Some gardeners in frost-free climates start seeds in May for fall and winter color.

Set plants out 9 inches apart in a sunny location of partial shade and rich, moist soil. Lobelia will take full sun if it gets enough water, but plants appear lusher and the flower color more intense in partial shade.

Among the compact varieties are 'Crystal Palace' (dark blue flowers), 'Cambridge Blue' (light blue), 'Mrs. Clibran' (dark blue flowers with white centers), and 'String of Pearls' (a mixture of colors). 'Sapphire' (azure blue) is trailing.

Madagascar Periwinkle

Catharanthus roseus, usually sold as *Vinca rosea.*
Photo on page 48.

Rugged, heat-loving, and smog-proof, Madagascar periwinkle (or simply vinca) is a very popular bedding or container plant in areas with long warm summers; it is the showiest flower in a desert garden. Madagascar periwinkle ranges from 1 to 2 feet tall, growing in rounded bushy plants with clusters of glossy, dark green leaves on sturdy stems. Each leaf cluster is centered by a phloxlike flower. Blossoms are pure white, white with red centers, pink with rose centers, and rose-pink. You can find them in single shades and mixed colors.

Use taller varieties as background for borders or in containers. For edgings and massed borders, you'll want the compact 10-inch plants: 'Bright Eyes,' white with a red eye, is a popular choice. 'Rose Carpet,' ideal for hanging baskets or for a groundcover, grows just 3 inches high and spreads to 24 inches. All types bloom from July to frost, and if you live in a frost-free area, your plants may live over; though grown as an annual, Madagascar periwinkle is a perennial.

Madagascar periwinkle grows slowly, so start seeds indoors except where summers are exceptionally long. Place the seeded flat in a plastic bag; seeds will sprout in 7 to 10 days in 70° heat. In cool-summer areas, plant seedlings in full sun outdoors; plant in part shade where heat is intense. If you prefer not to grow plants from seeds, buy them from the nursery. Place plants 6 to 12 inches apart to form solid beds and pinch off growing tips when they are 4 inches tall to make plants bush out. Keep soil moist, but don't overwater or the plants will become spindly. Feed once a month to keep foliage crisp. Madagascar periwinkle does not make a good cut flower.

Marigold

Tagetes species. Photo on page 48.

Of course you'll want marigolds, a flower as basic to gardens as sunshine; the only question is which types to grow. You have a wide selection to choose from. Flowers range in size from ¾-inch petites to 5-inch giants and come in single and mixed shades of maroon, orange, dark red, yellow, and combinations of these colors. Heights start at 6 inches and go all the way up to 3 feet.

Beginning gardeners prize marigolds for their quick and easy growth from seed, their resistance to pests, and their profusion of blooms throughout the summer and into fall. Experienced gardeners are charmed by the ever-new varieties of the flower, and they depend on the natural deterrent to nematodes that marigolds provide to neighboring plants.

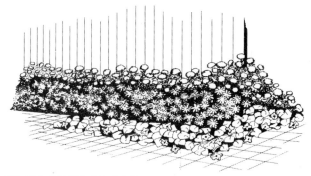

FROM HIGH TO LOW: marigolds (against fence) rise above dwarf dahlias; nasturtiums spill onto patio.

Use marigolds with a bold hand, massing them in drifts or bays. Try them with an edging of blue lobelia or ageratum. Grow them in containers or raised beds. Use them to fill in a blank spot among shrubs.

No annuals grow more easily from seed than marigolds. Large and easy to handle, the seeds usually germinate in about a week in warm soil. Seeds can be started in flats for early bloom, but many gardeners prefer to sow them directly in the ground where they are to grow.

Robust, free-blooming, and nearly trouble-free, marigolds like fair to good soil, full sun, and ample water and will bloom from early summer to frost if you pick off faded blossoms regularly. Avoid overhead watering: blossoms hold water like cups, and the weight may snap the brittle stems.

Be sure to plant the flowers the proper distance apart (see the seed packet) so that they will receive plenty of sunshine. Six inches between plants is usually enough for the smaller varieties, but big types may need as much as 18 inches.

The only objectionable feature of marigolds is a strong, sagelike scent. This odor has been bred out of some of the newer varieties. Marigolds make excellent, long-lasting cut flowers. If you bring a strong-smelling variety indoors, you can help cut down the aroma by adding a tablespoon of sugar to the water.

Marigolds fall into four main classes: African *(T. erecta),* French *(T. patula),* signet *(T. tenuifolia),* and triploid, a cross between French and African. Each class includes a host of strains and varieties.

African (or American) marigolds, often known as tall or semi-tall marigolds, produce large flowers (3 to 5 inches) on plants ranging from 12 to 36 inches tall depending on variety.

You'll probably find these African marigolds sold according to the name of the strain or series that they fall in. Some of the most common and popular of these are F_1 hybrids with carnationlike flowers: the Jubilee series, compact plants 2 feet tall with double flowers 3½ inches across; the Gold Coin series, 3½ to 4½-inch extra double flowers on 2½-foot plants; and the Climax series, 4 to 5-inch flowers on 3-foot plants. Varieties within each of these F_1 hybrid strains have double flowers in single or mixed colors of yellow, orange, and gold.

Other African types you might find are 'Crackerjack,' an early to mid-season bloomer with 3 to 4-inch double flowers in shades of orange, gold, and yellow; and 'Hawaii' which has odorless foliage and double 4-inch flowers.

Some African marigolds have chrysanthemumlike flowers: 'Glitters' is 2½ to 3 feet tall with 3-inch yellow blossoms; 'Spun Gold' and 'Spun Yellow' are only 12 inches tall with 2½ to 3-inch flowers in gold and yellow.

African marigolds prefer rich soil and frequent watering. If you buy them in flats, plant them deeply—allowing 2 to 3 inches of soil above the roots with soil around the first inch or two of the stem. (Remove foliage from the part of the stem to be covered.) If not planted deeply, they will need staking later on to remain upright. Encourage branching by pinching back when about 8 inches tall.

French marigolds are generally smaller both in flower and plant size than the Africans; they are excellent for edgings, borders, and containers, and many types have variegated or bicolored flowers.

Petite French marigold types are 6-inch mounding plants with 1-inch double flowers. 'Petite Yellow,' 'Petite Orange,' and 'Petite Gold' are clear solid colors; 'Petite Harmony'

is a bicolor with mahogany guard petals surrounding a gold crested center. 'Petite Mixed' is a blend of colors.

An Olé type French marigold, 'Bolero' grows 8 to 10 inches high and has large double carnation-type, bi-colored flowers in maroon and gold. 'Sparky' is another 8 to 10-inch bicolor in gold and red. The Cupid series is odorless with 2½-inch blooms on 10-inch plants in single and mixed colors. 'Brownie Scout,' 8 inches tall, has double flowers in yellow tinged with brownish red at the base. 'Naughty Marietta' has single flowers, 2½ inches across and golden yellow tinged with maroon at the base of each petal.

Signet marigolds have small single flowers in profuse bloom on 8-inch plants. 'Ursula' is gold with an orange center. Varieties in the Gem series have solid colors of gold or yellow.

The triploid marigolds are a cross between French and African types. They are "mules" in that the flowers are sterile and do not produce seeds. Because triploids do not go to seed, they bloom much more freely and for a longer period than either the French or African types. The F_1 hybrid Nugget triploid strain has double blooms 2 inches across on plants 12 inches tall. Nugget varieties have flowers in single and mixed colors.

Mignonette

Reseda odorata. Photo on page 50.

The beauty of mignonette lies mostly in its distinctive, sweet clean fragrance. The plant itself is 12 to 18 inches high, sprawling in growth habit, and rather weedy in appearance. The foliage is light green, and small yellow and white flowers grow in spiky clusters. You'll want to tuck mignonette into inconspicuous places as a filler in your garden —among other annuals, behind shrubs, in pots with other plants, or under a frequently open window that will let its fragrance drift indoors.

Sow seeds in warm soil outdoors; make successive sowings three weeks apart to assure your garden of fragrance throughout the summer. Mignonette grows quickly and, although it prefers full sun, it will take partial shade. Plants will bloom from spring through fall in mild climates. Extremely hot weather may dry up the blossoms.

Bring the fragrance indoors by massing cut spikes in a pottery bowl with other annuals. Cut blooms last for a week or more. The most fragrant varieties are 'Common Sweet Scented' and 'Machet.' 'Red Goliath' is a variety with larger flowers but less fragrance.

Mimulus

Mimulus species (Monkey flower). Photo on page 50.

A small plant with big flowers, mimulus will thrive at the shaded edge of a pool or where the soil is moist and ferns, violets, or bleeding hearts do well. During the blooming period, mimulus is covered with 2½-inch flowers brilliantly colored in gold, red, or yellow or strikingly mottled and variegated with brown or maroon.

M. cardinalis, a perennial grown as an annual, grows erect to 2½ feet. The slightly sticky leaves are 1 to 3 inches long and irregularly toothed.

(Continued on page 47)

IMPATIENS WALLERIANA

KOCHIA

LARKSPUR

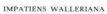

BALSAM

(Continued from page 45)

M. lewisii is a Western native growing to 1 to 2 feet with rather sloppy stems. The light green leaves are 1 to 4½ inches long, sharply toothed, and sticky.

M. tigrinus is a short-lived perennial with smooth, succulent, and toothed leaves. 'Queen's Prize' is a choice mixture of colors.

Mimulus is rather touchy about its cultural requirements—coolness, moist soil, and protection from direct sunlight (but not heavy shade). It makes an excellent pot plant. You can start mimulus from seeds indoors in January or February in 8-inch clay pots and take the small plants outside and sink them in the soil when danger of frost is past. In containers, plants will need frequent feeding and watering to stay healthy, but in the fall you can easily bring them indoors for winter bloom. Cut flowers will last 3 or 4 days in a cool room.

Morning Glory Vine

Ipomoea purpurea. Photo on page 50.

There's an exuberance about morning glory vines that makes you want to plant them where you can easily watch them grow and flower. The attractive foliage (large heart-shaped leaves) is dense enough to provide a temporary privacy screen. And you'll enjoy seeing the fresh display of large flowers opening daily—in shades of blue, crimson, magenta, pink, or white—all summer long.

To hasten germination of the hard seeds, nick the corner with a file. Plant them in full sun outdoors or start in peat pots indoors and transplant when the frost danger is past. Keep plants moist, but do not overwater or overfeed or you'll get more foliage and fewer flowers.

The vines require training to climb up fences, trellises, or walls. Use sturdy string, wire, or light rope netting. For arrangements, pick stems with flowers and buds in different stages of development.

Among the varieties, 'Early Call' has large rose colored flowers with white throats. 'Heavenly Blue' ranks as a top favorite. It is sky blue, shading to cream in the center. 'Pearly Gates' (All-America) is early blooming and pure white. Morning glories also come in mixed colors.

Nasturtium

Tropaeolum majus. Photo on page 50.

Free-blooming, colorful, long-lasting, and so easy to grow that in parts of the country it thrives as a wildflower, nasturtium is a perfect flower for the beginning gardener and a boon to the expert. Besides, its leaves and flowers are good to eat! They have a peppery, watercress flavor that adds bite to a salad and zest to a pot of soup. (Caution: do not eat the seeds—they, can be poisonous.) If you give nasturtiums sun and sandy, well-drained soil, their distinctive round, shield-shaped leaves and bright sturdy flowers will grow rapidly to cover the ground or sparkle in window boxes. Blossoms, about 2 inches across and single or double petalled, come in a wide range of single shades and bicolors—from root-beer brown and maroon through reds, oranges, and yellows to pure cream.

Trailing types found in the Gleam strain can be trained on trellises and will climb to 6 feet; some bush-shaped dwarfs and compact types such as the Jewel Mixture grow only 8 to 15 inches tall. Both the trailing and compact dwarf kinds make good ground covers. You can find seed packets of nasturtiums with double or single flowers in mixed colors and single shades.

Nasturtium seeds are as large as peas and only need to be poked into the ground, ½ to 1 inch deep; children will find them a rewarding first flower. Some of the seed varieties come hulled for faster germination. If you get seeds with hulls, give them a good soaking in water for a few hours before planting.

Nasturtiums do not transplant well, so plant the seeds in a permanent location. While plants prefer full sun and poor soil, they will grow in shade and rich soil but there they'll produce more leaves and fewer flowers.

You may find nasturtiums tasty, but so do aphids. Spraying with a non-detergent soap solution, especially on the undersides of the leaves where aphids hide, will usually take care of the problem. Rinse sprayed foliage and flowers thoroughly before eating them.

Nemesia

Nemesia strumosa. Photo on page 52.

Brilliant delicate flowers massed on short bushy plants distinguish this cool-weather annual. Nemesia blooms from early summer until heat kills it off. The flowers, ¾ inch across, bloom on 3-inch spikes that lift them above the foliage. Flowers come in almost every color but green. Nemesia makes an excellent edging, a first-rate bulb cover, and is spectacular in containers. It looks particularly splendid combined with lobelia or violas around a patio. A dwarf variety, 'Nana Compacta' grows 10 inches tall. Most seed packets contain mixed colors.

Where winters are mild, plant nemesia outdoors in full sun in fall or very early spring. Elsewhere, plant outdoors in full sun when the danger of frost is past. When plants are 6 inches high, pinch off the tips of the tallest branches to get compact plants. Keep soil moist but not soggy; apply fertilizer regularly for abundant bloom. A little protection from afternoon sun will prolong the blooming period. A fine cut flower, nemesia makes lively arrangements.

Nicotiana

Nicotiana alata (Flowering tobacco). Photo on page 52.

The sweet fragrance and ample loose clusters of trumpet-shaped blossoms that distinguish nicotiana make it a flower worth waiting for. And wait you will, for the seeds take about a month to sprout.

Originally nicotiana was an evening bloomer, remaining closed on all but cloudy days, but strains such as Sensation Mixed have flowers that open in daylight. Plants vary from 1 to 3 feet tall, with flowers in crimson, lavender, lime, maroon, mauve, or white and large hairy leaves near the base. Nicotiana looks best in groups of 4 to 6 plants. Use

LINARIA

MADAGASCAR PERIWINKLE

LOBELIA

MARIGOLD 'PETITE YELLOW'

it as an upright accent among lower growing summer-blooming flowers.

In short-summer areas, start seeds indoors in flats or buy your plants from the nursery. In areas with a long growing season, plant the seeds in the garden in early spring. Broadcast them over the planting area but do not cover with soil. Once seeds have sprouted, plants develop rapidly.

Nicotiana tolerates considerable heat if given some shade in the afternoon. In cooler areas, it thrives in full sun or part shade. It is a good choice for window boxes, where its scent will perfume the house.

When cut, flowers last for 3 or 4 days—new blossoms open daily to replace yesterday's. Cut whole stems while the flowers are in full bloom and place in deep water.

Nigella

Nigella damascena (Love-in-a-mist).
Photo on page 52.

Nigella has a double charm: first, as a fresh, lacy summer flower and second, when blooming is over in the fall, as an unusual addition to dried bouquets. Easy to grow and reaching a height of 1 to 2 feet, nigella is cherished for its fine airy foliage, its blue, rose, or white-colored flowers centered in a corona of greenery, and its spiky seed pods. Blossoms are borne singly on the ends of the branches. Nigella is best as a grace note among taller, sturdier annuals.

In fall or early spring, sow seeds in full sun where plants are to remain. Nigella comes into bloom quickly and begins to dry up in late summer; you can prolong its flowering with regular watering.

As cut flowers, nigella adds delicacy to bouquets of spring flowering bulbs. 'Miss Jekyll,' a cornflower blue, is a prized variety.

Pansy

Viola species. Photos on page 53.

Among the many members of the violet genus, two species are particular favorites of flower gardeners everywhere—the pansy and viola.

Pansies and violas are perennials grown as annuals, and to all but the most careful observer, they are practically indistinguishable. In culture, the two are so similar that they are included in the same discussion below.

Pansies (Viola tricolor hortensis) have both mixed and single-colored flowers. A blotch of color in the center of multicolored flowers often resembles a cat's face and, for many gardeners, is the pansy's most endearing and distinguishing feature. Plants are short and compact (seldom exceeding 8 inches in height), with the trend in cultivated varieties towards larger flowers—up to 4 inches across. Varieties of the Swiss Giant strain are popular. They have large flowers in many colors and color groupings.

Violas (Viola cornuta) usually have solid-colored flowers, generally smaller than those of pansies. Violas also form more tufted, mounding plants than do pansies. Among the varieties are 'Blue Perfection' (medium blue), 'Arkwright Ruby' (bright red with a dark center), and 'Lutea Splendens,' a golden yellow.

Harbingers of spring, dainty pansies and violas are tougher than they look. Pollution-resistant, they are a favorite plant for city street-side containers, edgings, fillers in perennial borders, and accompaniments for spring bulbs. Light frost won't damage them, and some of the newer strains will even brave full sun to bloom well into summer.

Though sturdy as adults, pansies and violas are difficult infants, and you may find it easiest to buy small plants in flats or pots from the nursery. If you do plan to grow them from seeds, start early. In cold-winter areas, begin your seeds indoors in midwinter. If you live in an area where winters are mild, you can start seeds in July or August; you'll be rewarded with some bloom in the fall, maybe a little during the winter, and an all-out performance through the entire spring.

To grow compact, free-blooming pansies, plant them in an area with at least full morning sun. Soil should be crumbly, loamy, rich, and well drained. Water plants in flats thoroughly the day before you transplant them to loosen the soil in the planting blocks and to make sure water will be easily available to the roots. Set plants in the ground at exactly the same depth they were in the flat. If you want a massed or groundcover effect, space pansies 8 inches apart. Water after planting. Keep the roots cool in the summer with a light mulch.

For perfect pansies, feed them generously—diluted liquid fertilizer every 3 or 4 weeks—and water thoroughly. Never let pansies dry out; keep the ground loose and the roots cool in the summer. Pinch pansies back if they are leggy. Keep blooms picked off until plants are established; once they are in full bloom, pick as often as you can. Pansies make fine cut flowers and will keep 3 or 4 days in deep water. It's best to cut long stems with buds and leaves.

You may need to defend your pansies from aphids with a good contact-type insecticide and from snails and slugs with bait. Birds will fly off with very tiny plants; protect them indoors until they are rooted enough to hold their own.

Petunia

Petunia hybrida. Photo on page 53.

The ideal container plant, the perfect edging for a flower bed, and the choice brightener for a mass of shrubs, petunias rank with marigolds and zinnias as the flower gardener's favorite. The trumpet-shaped single and double blossoms with their pleasing fragrance and delightful profusion come in virtually every color, and many bicolors.

Because petunias thrive in almost all temperate climates, they offer a big advantage over many annuals if you're looking for color. In most areas, they bloom throughout the summer; in desert areas, they'll blossom from October through May.

You can easily grow petunias from seeds sown in flats or in the open ground in well-prepared soil. Seeds are tiny and should be mixed with fine sand before sowing to insure even distribution. Because they take a little more time from seed to flower than most annuals, you'll want to start them 10 weeks prior to your first frost-free date if summers are short in your area.

Many gardeners prefer to skip the initial fuss of seeds and buy young plants from the nursery. If you choose this

NASTURTIUM

MIGNONETTE

MORNING GLORY VINE

MIMULUS

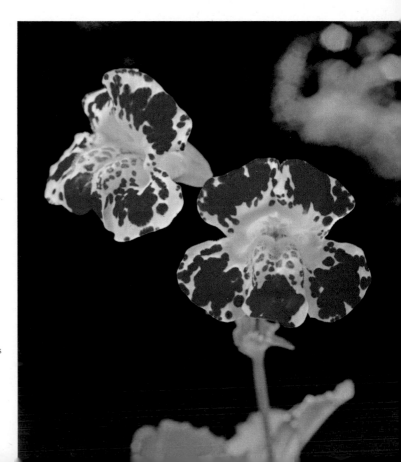

50

shortcut, be sure to get young, sturdy seedlings; avoid leggy, woody, half-grown plants which won't perform well.

For best growth, space your plants 8 to 18 inches apart, depending on the variety you're growing. You'll get the best results in full sun, but petunias also do well in part shade. Any good garden soil or planting mix is fine; single-flowered types thrive even in poor soil.

Once established, petunias do not need large amounts of water, but for maximum performance, give them an occasional dose of fertilizer. When young plants are 6 inches high, pinch them back to promote side branching. At mid-summer, many plants may begin to look straggly; at this time, cut them back to about 6 inches high, fertilize, and soak well with water—in a week or two they'll start behaving like new plants.

Petunias perform strongly in dry climates; but in humid areas they may pick up botrytis disease which disfigures blossoms and foliage. If you live in a humid region, look for types marked "botrytis resistant" on the seed packet, usually among the F₁ Hybrid Multifloras.

Cut petunias last for several days if you pick off faded blooms regularly: you'll have the best luck with single-flower types. Mass the cut flowers in small bowls or combine them with phlox and baby's breath.

You have dozens of named varieties of petunias to choose from, and plant breeders are continually introducing new ones each year. Most of these fall into either the F₁ Hybrid Grandiflora class or the F₁ Hybrid Multiflora class.

F₁ Hybrid Grandiflora petunias are vigorous plants growing from 15 to 27 inches high and 24 to 26 inches across. Flowers are either single or double, often fringed or ruffled, and very large—up to 5 inches across. Flowers are white, yellow, salmon, crimson, red, blue, or purple in single shades, bicolors, and mixed colors.

The double-flowered varieties are very lovely, but plants are often weak and difficult to start. The Magic series has single flowers with clean solid colors on early blooming plants. The Cascade series features single flowers on flowing stems that are especially good in hanging containers and window boxes.

Varieties in the F₁ Hybrid Multiflora class are about the same size as those in the F₁ Hybrid Grandiflora class, but the double or single flowers are generally smooth-edged and smaller (to 2 inches across). They have a neat compact growth form that makes them ideal for bedding and massed plantings. Multifloras are often resistant to botrytis disease. They feature the same colors as the Grandifloras.

The Satin series has single, 2½-inch-wide flowers with

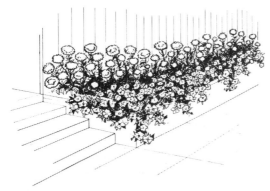

RAISED PLANTING BED along a sunny walk is perfect for zinnias and cascading petunias (foreground).

a satiny texture and a wide selection of colors. The Tart series is double-flowered.

The Giants of California strain features the largest flowers. Heavily ruffled with open, often veined throats, the blooms average 5 to 6 inches across. Colors include salmon, deep rose, wine-red, magenta, orchid, and white. Their real place is in containers and raised beds, but they can also be massed in borders.

Phlox, annual

Phlox drummondii (Pride of Texas).
Photo on page 53.

Showy and abundant clusters of blossoms held well above bushy foliage characterize this native Texas flower. Phlox comes in an interesting range of sizes—from 6 to 18 inches—with flowers in single and combined colors of lavender, pink, red, white, and yellow. Some types have frilled or starred flowers with contrasting edgings and eyes.

Seeds germinate best in cool soil: sow them outdoors during cool weather either in the fall or spring. Or start seeds in flats indoors during the winter. Where summers are long and hot, phlox is used as a spring flower to fill in between young cleome, marigolds, and zinnias. In cool-summer areas, phlox will bloom until early fall.

Phlox is attractive in arrangements for 2 to 3 days if you pick off individual flowers as they shrivel. Mass them alone or combine them with other flowers, such as marigolds and zinnias of harmonious colors.

Among the varieties, those in the Giant Tetra Improved (tetraploid) and Gigantea Art Shades strains have the largest flowers and grow to about 1 foot. Dwarf types such as 'Stellata Twinkle' (All-America), with starlike two-tone flowers, grow just 6 inches high.

Pincushion Flower

Scabiosa atropurpurea (Mourning bride).
Photo on page 55.

A giant among annuals, pincushion flower grows 2 to 4 feet tall and will give you multi-rayed, dome-shaped flowers throughout the summer. The 2-inch-wide flowers with long slender stems, studded with protruding stamens that look exactly like pins in a cushion, come in a multitude of velvety colors ranging from white through blues and reds to maroon. Pincushion flower makes a good background plant for phlox or other dense-growing flowers. When cut, their blossoms keep for several days.

Pincushion flower is easy to grow and thrives in most areas except where summers are extremely hot. Sow seeds in warm soil and full sun outdoors where plants are to remain. When massed, they will look less spindly, and the heavy blossom heads will be less likely to droop. Pinching off tip branches will encourage bushier growth. Remove flowers as they fade.

Pincushion flower comes in single colors and mixtures. 'Heavenly Blue' has lavender-blue flowers on compact, 18-inch plants; 'Black Night' is taller with reddish black flowers. 'Fire King' is scarlet; 'Peach Blossom,' pink. Dwarf Mixed is a compact strain growing 10 inches tall.

NICOTIANA

NIGELLA

NEMESIA

PANSY

VIOLA

PETUNIA 'WHITE CASCADE'

PHLOX

53

Poppy

Papaver species. Photos on page 55.

Poppies come in a variety of annual and perennial versions, all with cup-shaped flowers formed by crinkly silken petals and all easy to grow. Most frequently cultivated are the Shirley poppy, a true annual and the Iceland poppy, a perennial grown as an annual in warm-winter climates for winter and early spring bloom. (The California poppy is not a true poppy; see page 32.)

Shirley poppy (strains of corn poppy, *P. rhoeas*) bears its flowers on slender, 2-foot-high stems in spring or early summer in cool regions. For continuous bloom, you can plant batches of seeds successively. Numerous blossoms open from pendulous fat buds in a very short time. The single or double flowers come in shades of pink, rose, salmon, scarlet, and white; you can buy seeds for single and mixed-colored flowers. Two solid color varieties are 'Sweet Briar,' with deep rose-pink double flowers, and 'American Legion,' with large scarlet single flowers.

Iceland poppy *(P. nudicaule)* is a perennial grown as an annual for winter and spring bloom in warm-winter areas; if sown in earliest spring, it will produce summer bloom in cool areas. Iceland poppy is somewhat more substantial and has a longer blooming period than Shirley poppy. Stems grow 18 inches high and are topped by orange, pink, scarlet, white, and yellow flowers. Gartford Giant strain is a mixture of large double flowers; Pink Champagne is a warm pink; Champagne Bubbles, an F_1 hybrid, has large flowers in a wide range of colors on bushy 15-inch plants.

Plant both Shirley and Iceland poppy seeds by mixing them with sand and scattering in the garden. Seeds sprout quickly in cool soil and are best planted in masses so you'll always have fresh color coming. Transplanting is chancy; both kinds do best in full sun and in ordinary garden soil outdoors. The young leaves in basal rosettes are delicious to birds, so cover small plants with wire or cloth netting. Charming cut flowers, poppies should be picked when buds first show color. Sear the ends of the flower stems or dip them in boiling water to seal in the juices, and then place them in a deep container of cold water.

Portulaca

Portulaca grandiflora (Rose moss). Photo on page 55.

Brilliant, hardy, and easy to grow, portulaca is an ideal temporary ground cover for sunny rock gardens or driveway strips. The vivid flowers, about 1½ inches across, look like single or double roses in lavender, magenta, orange, red, white, and yellow and are profusely borne on succulent plants only 6 inches high but spreading to 18 inches. Flowers close in the late afternoon and on cloudy days.

Heat tolerant and drought resistant, portulaca thrives in sandy soil and full sun and requires very little watering. But it does just as well in areas where summers are short and cool.

If you live in an area where summers are long and hot, plant portulaca seeds in warm soil and full sun after all danger of frost is past. The seeds are fine: mix them with sand and sprinkle in garden rows spaced 14 inches apart.

Press the soil down firmly; the seeds will work their own way into the ground and won't germinate if planted too deeply. Keep the soil moist until seeds sprout. For early bloom, start seeds indoors 2 months before the average date of the last frost. If you place the seeded flat in a warm spot (70 to 75°), seeds should germinate in 7 to 10 days.

Salpiglossis

Salpiglossis sinuata (Painted tongue).
Photo on page 58.

Related to petunia, salpiglossis is prized for its rich colors, unusual markings, and its excellence as a cut flower. The velvety, 2 to 3-inch, trumpet-shaped flowers are borne on 2 to 3-foot plants. Flower colors are blue, gold, mahogany, red-orange, and scarlet; flowers in the Emperor strain are traced with pencil-fine markings in contrasting shades and are interesting in mass plantings.

Salpiglossis is difficult to start from seeds. If you want to try, put several seeds in potting mix in peat pots during late winter or early spring. Keep the mix moist and the pots in a warm, protected location. Seeds should sprout in 7 to 10 days. Thin to one seedling per pot. When young plants are well established, plant them outdoors after all danger of frost is past.

Salpiglossis does best in a sunny spot in the garden with rich soil and protection from the wind. Be careful not to overwater: plants should receive generous watering in the beginning and less water as they grow. The slender stems are weak and may need propping. Pinch out tips of growing plants to encourage branching. Plants bloom from late spring until frost.

Salvia

See Scarlet sage.

Scarlet Runner Bean Vine

Phaseolus coccineus. Photo on page 58.

This fast-growing annual vine has the happy property of producing both colorful flowers and beans that are edible when young and green. Although basically a vegetable, scarlet runner bean vine carries sprays of bright scarlet sweet pea-shaped blossoms so attractive that the vine is often used for screening and for covering fences.

Sow the seeds in spring after frosts. The purple and black-mottled seeds are quite large; they germinate in about 4 days in warm soil. Vines climb to 6 to 10 feet by mid-summer; like sunflowers and nasturtiums, they're easy plants for children to grow.

Scarlet runner bean vine is subject to the usual garden pests; spray or dust with multipurpose insecticide. The bean pods are dark green, long, and flattened. Since they become tough and fibrous with age, they should be eaten when about 4 inches long.

ICELAND POPPY

PINCUSHION FLOWER

PORTULACA

SHIRLEY POPPY

Scarlet Sage

Salvia splendens, often sold as *Salvia.*
Photo on page 58.

Flower-laden spikes of dazzling red rise above the dark green foliage of scarlet sage, making an exclamation point of color in your garden. The red is very strong and usually overpowers other garden colors; you will enjoy scarlet sage most against a background of green or gray foliage or in the background among purple or white petunias, snow-on-the-mountain, or daisies. Scarlet sage grows to heights of 8 to 30 inches, and the flowers are shades of red—from rose-red to orange-red. You may also find lavender-blue and white varieties, though the reds are most common.

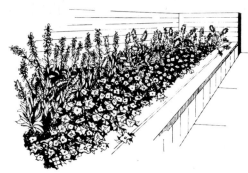

BRIGHT RED scarlet sage makes a strikingly elegant background for a border of purple or white petunias.

Scarlet sage takes longer to grow than most annuals. You can get a head start by germinating seeds in flats indoors in February or March. Keep the flats in direct sun and the temperature at about 70°. Transplant seedlings into the garden when the soil warms. Rather than grow plants from seeds, you may prefer to buy flats of scarlet sage from the nursery. Scarlet sage prefers direct sun but will tolerate partial shade.

Expect a continuous blaze of color from June until frost but don't try to bring the blossoms indoors: they do not survive cutting. Among the red varieties, 'St. John's Fire,' an early-blooming dwarf about 12 inches high, and 'Early Bonfire,' 2 to 3 feet tall, are popular.

Schizanthus

See Butterfly flower.

Snapdragon

Antirrhinum majus. Photo on page 58.

Long-time favorites that contribute vertical form to the spring garden, snapdragons bloom throughout the summer in mild-summer areas. Their warm, rich, velvety colors, their spikes of single or double flowers, and their range of heights (4 inches to 4 feet) give snapdragons a place in practically all gardens.

Most gardeners sow snapdragon seeds in flats indoors during late fall and winter and set out the young plants in early spring. Although seeds can be planted directly in the garden in the spring, they dry out easily and require frequent watering with a fine spray. If you need only a few "snaps," you'll find sturdy young plants at nurseries.

Plant snapdragons in full sun if possible and in moderately rich, well-drained soil. Space tall kinds 18 inches apart, bedding types 10 inches apart, and the very miniature varieties 6 inches apart. Be generous with water. If you live in a windy area, stake tall plants to keep them upright.

For maximum bloom, cut the flower spikes often; they are long lasting as cut flowers and combine well with delphiniums, roses, and dahlias. When your plants begin to look tired and bloomed out, cut them back drastically and give them a dose of liquid fertilizer.

Rust is snapdragon's most serious disease and can develop quickly. You can easily recognize it by the dusty, dark brown spots that appear on the underside of the leaves and on the stem. To inhibit rust, dust every 2 weeks with sulphur, starting early in the season, or spray with a fungicide. Avoid getting the leaves wet when you water.

You can find snapdragons in a wide variety of colors—both single and mixed—and types that range from 4 to 6 inches high to 4 feet high. Both single and double flowered types are available. An "unsnapped" type (peloric or butterfly flowered) is sold as 'Bright Butterflies.'

Snow-on-the-Mountain

Euphorbia marginata. Photo on page 60.

A cousin of the poinsettia, snow-on-the-mountain is loved for its leaves which are oval-shaped, light green, and striped and margined with white. Plants grow 2 to 3 feet high. They blend well with other plants in perennial borders and make a fine background for such brilliant blooms as scarlet sage and zinnias.

Easy to grow, snow-on-the-mountain self-sows so readily that it may become a weed if you don't pick the flowers before they ripen and drop seeds. Sow seeds outdoors in warm soil and full sun. Expect rapid growth.

Handle cuttings with great care if you want to bring them indoors for foliage with other cut flowers: the sap is poisonous and can irritate the skin. Wear gloves and seal cut ends with a flame or by dipping them in boiling water for a few minutes. Combine the foliage in bouquets with marigolds and dahlias.

Statice

Limonium (Sea lavender). Photo on page 60.

Here is a late-summer bloomer with open clusters of blossoms on short, one-sided spikes. Statice has blue, purple, rose, and yellow flowers on 2-foot stems rising from a dense clump of large basal leaves. It makes a superb dried flower, keeping its colors extremely well.

As a wildflower, statice is found in meadows and hills by the sea, thriving on salt spray. If you live near the ocean, you'll particularly enjoy its hardiness; inland, grow statice in any well-drained soil and full sun.

Sow seeds outdoors in early spring where plants are to grow and do not over water. (Statice does best when kept on the dry side.) For earliest bloom, start seeds in flats 8 weeks before final spring frost. Take great care not to damage the long tap roots while transplanting.

Stock

Matthiola incana. Photo on page 60.

A favorite with American gardeners since the days of George Washington (when it was known as the gilliflower), stock is a fragrant and colorful annual. The straight or branching stems, 1 to 3 feet tall and crowned with spikes of single or double blossoms, make stock an effective bedding flower and good in mass plantings. You can find it in mixed colors or in single shades of lavender, magenta, pink, purple, rose, white, and yellow, each carrying a unique spicy fragrance. Stock makes a superb and long-lasting cut flower.

The type of stock you should grow depends on where you live. The Giant Imperial and Column types, tall-growing (2 feet) and spectacular as cut flowers, are recommended only for areas with mild winters. Sow seed outdoors directly where you want them to grow; the long winter vegetative period will prepare them for spring bloom.

Dwarf Ten Weeks and Trysomic Seven Weeks types can be grown successfully in either mild or cold climates. The best way to grow them is to seed very early (at sweet pea time) in spring, outdoors. Sow the seeds thickly; later on, do not thin or feed the young plants. This forces an early blooming period, and they will stay in bloom until early July.

Any interruption of growth can have serious consequences. If you sow seed in flats, be sure to set out the young plants before they become flatbound. (Stock is a popular item in nurseries; you'll do best if you shop for it early.)

A sunny location is best, but light shade is acceptable in hot climates. Soil should be light, fertile, and well drained. Stock should be watered regularly, but stems will rot if water is allowed to collect in pools at the base of the plants. If you have heavy soil, you'll get best results by planting in raised beds.

Strawflower

Helichrysum bracteatum. Photo on page 60.

Meet one of the best everlastings. Strawflower has glistening, 2½-inch-wide, pomponlike flower heads with colorful, papery, petal-like bracts in orange, red, white, or yellow. A sturdy, 2 to 3-foot plant having numerous long stems, it is especially good for cutting. Although it can be used in borders, strawflower is too coarse to be featured up front.

Strawflower is easy to grow. Plant the seeds in late spring or early summer just as you would zinnias or marigolds. This annual needs full sun and is adapted to all but extremely hot climates. It will grow successfully in dry soil.

The colorful flowers are good when fresh in arrangements. If you wish to dry them, cut the flowers before the yellow centers (disc flowers) show; strip off the leaves and bundle each color separately; wrap the bundles in a newspaper cone and hang them upside down in a dry, shady place.

The Dwarf Double Mixed strain grows about 18 inches to 2 feet tall and has a wide range of flower colors including shades of crimson, gold, pink, ruby, white, and yellow. It is earlier blooming than the taller growing strawflowers.

Sunflower

Helianthus annuus. Photo on page 61.

Sunflower's characteristically thick, upright stalk grows so high that the *dwarf* strain is 3 feet tall. Best-known is the Russian type that quickly grows to 6 feet in cool windy areas and to 10 to 15 feet when planted on the warm sheltered side of a house or fence. The blossoms at the tops of the stalks grow from 5 to 10 inches across, with rayed yellow flowers and centers of gold, orange, or mahogany. The leaves are often 12 inches long.

Easy to grow, sunflowers are a favorite with children. Plant sunflower seeds outdoors in full sun in any warm soil, water twice a week, and watch the plants shoot up towards the sky. For extra-fast growth, fertilize occasionally.

The seeds, which form by the hundreds in the flower heads, are delicious to eat and are a good source of niacin. Place the seeds in a single layer in a large pan and toast them in the oven at 250° for 20 minutes, then crack the outside shell and eat the meat.

Among varieties, 'Teddy Bear' is a double golden flower on a 3-foot plant; 'Sungold' is a medium height (7 feet) double; 'Mammoth' is a giant single-flowered variety.

Sweet Pea

Lathyrus odoratus. Photo on page 61.

Ever since they were first brought to America out of their native Sicily nearly 300 years ago, these hardy climbing annuals have been a favorite with gardeners.

Sweet pea's popularity is readily understandable when you consider some of their outstanding characteristics: you can get them in any color except yellow; the flowers are attractive, delightfully fragrant, and superb for cutting; and they bloom in great profusion during the spring and well into summer.

Fresh, dainty, fragrant, and long-stemmed, sweet peas can provide a profuse supply of cut flowers. Everything done in cultivating them is directed to perfect the individual flower rather than to produce a mass of color in the garden.

There are several kinds of sweet peas. Vine type sweet peas include multifloras, which are the earliest to flower, and floribundas, which bloom in late spring. Bijou sweet peas are dwarfs that grow 12 inches high, work well in containers, and need little support for their vines. Knee-Hi and bush types are strong vines that will support themselves and grow to 30 inches. All types make excellent cut flowers.

If you live in a mild-winter region, the best time to plant sweet peas is in late summer for early winter flowers or in early winter for early spring blooms. In cold-winter areas, sow seeds outdoors in early spring as soon as the ground is dry enough to be worked. Or start seeds indoors in peat pots 6 to 8 weeks before the last frost. You can save yourself much of the struggle of growing sweet peas if you buy small plants from the nursery.

(Continued on page 59)

SCARLET SAGE

SNAPDRAGON

SCARLET RUNNER BEAN VINE

SALPIGLOSSIS

(Continued from page 57)

To prepare the garden soil for seeds, dig an 18-inch-deep trench and refill it with soil mixed with humus and steer manure, adding fertilizer to the top 6 inches.

Soak the seeds for several hours in warm water to soften the seed coat. Before planting, shake the seeds in a bag with powdered fungicide. Plant the seeds in single or double rows, an inch deep and an inch apart, within a 2-inch-deep trench that will serve as a water-holding basin. Since Knee-Hi types grow very well in ordinary prepared seed beds, it is not necessary to dig a water trench for them.

Erect a screen over the young plants to protect them from birds; set out bait for slugs and snails. If you choose the most common vine-type sweet pea, be sure to construct a trellis immediately so the vines can find support as soon as the first tendrils reach out. You can make your own out of strands of coarse string tied 6 inches apart to a lath frame. In cool regions you can use chicken wire; but where summers are hot, the wire will heat up and cook the vines. Be sure to give the sweet pea vines plenty of air if mildew is a problem.

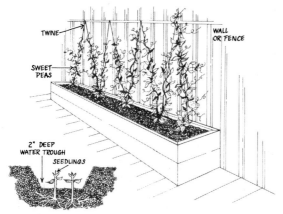

SWEET PEAS can be grown from seeds in wooden box. Twine going from fence to soil provides climbing support.

During the active growth period, apply a top dressing that is low in nitrogen but high in potash and phosphates. Water deeply and frequently.

To prolong the blooming period, pick sweet peas every couple of days to prevent the seed pods from ripening.

Sweet Sultan

Centaurea moschata. Photo on page 61.

A splendid cutting flower, sweet sultan is a cousin to bachelor's button, and, like that relative, is not noted for beautiful foliage. Plants are branching to 2 feet tall with dark green, deeply toothed leaves and lightly scented thistlelike flowers that are 2 inches across and lilac, purple, rose, white, or yellow in color. Sweet sultan looks best in drifts among other spring and early-summer blooming plants, such as white candytuft or cynoglossum.

Plants grow fairly rapidly. Sow the seeds in the fall unless your winters are quite severe, then sow them as early as possible. Seeds can be broadcast on roughly prepared beds; spring rains will wash them into the soil. Plant seeds in full sun.

Sweet William

See *Dianthus.*

Tithonia

Tithonia rotundifolia (Mexican sunflower).
Photo on page 61.

Tall bright tithonia is at its best in August and September when the weather is hot and dry. A desert native, it has 3 to 6-foot stalks and vivid red-orange, 3-inch flowers that are good in the background along a fence or sunny wall where the plants have plenty of room to grow. The robust, coarse-leaved plants spread as high as they are wide.

Plant seeds in warm soil outdoors and, after they've sprouted, thin the seedlings to 4 feet apart so they'll have room to spread. In cold-winter areas, plant seeds indoors in pots during the winter. By the time the frost danger is past, you'll have 8 to 12-inch plants ready to set out for August bloom. If you seed directly in the ground in cold climates, plants won't bloom until September. Tithonia takes plenty of sun and light water.

Cut flowers must be handled carefully since stalks are hollow and brittle and blossoms break off easily. Like marigolds, sunflowers, and zinnias, tithonia's flowers look best in massed arrangements by themselves, perhaps with a filler of baby's breath or statice. 'Torch' is a popular variety.

Torenia

Torenia fournieri (Wishbone flower).
Photo on page 63.

A charming but little known plant, torenia is easy to grow and fine for summer and fall bloom in partial shade. The compact bushy plants grow to 1 foot high and have bronzy green foliage. The gloxinialike flowers (white or sky blue with violet lower lips and yellow throats) are borne in profusion and have stamens that resemble a wishbone.

Torenia grows well in all 50 states. Only where summers are cool and short should it be grown in full sun. Plant torenia in warm soil where it is to remain; its seeds won't sprout until the soil is quite warm. For earlier bloom, start seeds indoors; seedlings transplant easily. Plants like plenty of humidity; blossoms tend to fade where the air is dry.

An informal planting of torenia on the fringes of a grove of trees is most attractive. Or try them in containers in half shade. Combine with edgings of lobelia or fibrous begonia or plant with a background of ferns. In hanging baskets, use torenia with trailing lobelia. The blossoms are short lived in arrangements.

Verbena

Verbena hybrida, usually sold as *V. hortensis.*
Photo on page 63.

Prized for its beauty, scent, and long blooming period, verbena is a perennial grown as an annual, with abundant

SNOW-ON-THE-MOUNTAIN

STATICE

STOCK

STRAWFLOWER

60

SUNFLOWER

SWEET PEA

SWEET SULTAN

TITHONIA

flowers the first year. Its flowers appear in flat, compact clusters, 2 to 3 inches wide, on plants 6 to 10 inches high that spread 18 inches to 2 feet wide. Colors range from pastel to deep shades of violet, red, and cream, with some blossoms having white centers.

Drought-resistant and heat-loving, verbena is a fine choice for parking strips and for along dry banks and walls.

Sow seeds in warm soil outdoors. Where summers are short, seeds should be started indoors. (Seedlings are a little slow to start indoors and need warmth and ample light for good growth.) Give verbena full sun, and plenty of water.

Cut whole branches for bouquets; they'll last 2 or 3 days indoors, and plants quickly grow new stems to replace those you take. You can find verbena in both mixtures and in solid colors in a variety of heights. Plants of the Rainbow Mixture, an 8 to 14-inch dwarf form, bloom earliest.

Vinca Rosea

See Madagascar periwinkle.

Viola

See Pansy.

Virginian Stock

Malcolmia maritima. Photo on page 63.

If you live in a cool-weather area and want a quick show of spring flowers, try Virginian stock. It often blooms just 6 weeks after you plant seeds. The only resemblance Virginian stock has to garden stock is its flower colors—cream, lavender, magenta, pink, rose, and white. Single stemmed or branching from the base, Virginian stock grows 6 to 8 inches high and is covered with nearly scentless 4-petaled flowers. It effectively covers out-of-bloom bulb beds, rocky outcroppings, or natural meadows.

Sow seeds in the early spring where plants are to remain. Full sun is preferred, but Virginian stock grows so fast that plants bloom under deciduous trees before the trees leaf out. The faintly fragrant flowers in small clusters show off best in dense bouquets.

Zinnia

Zinnia elegans. Photo on page 63.

The flamboyant zinnia comes in sizes, forms, and heights so diverse and interesting that you could fill your whole garden with them and never become bored. Just give zinnias sun, good soil, and plenty of water (but not overhead water, which will weight them down and snap off the flower heads, as well as burn the foliage and encourage mildew), and they'll entertain you all summer long. Though there are no blue zinnias, they do come in every other color and combination of colors. Flower sizes range from less than an inch to 7 inches across, with rays arranged in small neat rows or in shaggy heads on plants from 6 inches to 3 feet

tall. Zinnias are long-lasting and attractive cut flowers.

Zinnias bloom quickly and easily from seed in about 8 weeks, depending on the variety. Successive sowings in mild climates will give you flowers from early summer to frost.

In spring or early summer, plant the large seeds in full sun and in a warm location. It's best to choose a location where air circulation is good; here your zinnias will have a better chance of escaping their one bugaboo—mildew. Place the seeds 4 inches apart and bury them no more than ¼ inch deep. Press the soil down firmly. Seeds should germinate in 4 to 6 days.

Do not overwater the seedlings. Don't let them dry out entirely, but do keep them on the "dry" side to prevent damping off disease. When plants are about 4 inches high, thin the larger types to a distance of half their final height.

If you buy zinnia transplants at a nursery, look for young ones that have not begun to flower or set buds. Unless transplanted with care, flat-started zinnias and nursery plants will suffer some setback when planted out. When transplanting, be sure to block plants out so that the roots don't get exposed to drying air; water immediately and provide temporary shade if the weather is warm.

When the first buds form, pinch them off to stimulate lateral growth and more abundant flowers. Water zinnias frequently from below and feed them about once a month with a complete fertilizer.

Even if you give zinnias model care—keeping your plants in full sun, spacing them properly, and watering them carefully—you may get some mildew towards the end of the summer. Dusting with a fungicide when plants are young will help some, but often your best course is simply to destroy the affected plants.

Among the many varieties available in a wide range of single and mixed colors, the Giant Cactus Flowered types growing 2 to 2½ feet tall with double flowers 4 to 5 inches across and gracefully curved and quilled are some of the largest. Zenith, an F_1 hybrid, is a large cactus-flowered type with 5½ to 6-inch flowers in mixed and single colors on bushy plants. 'Carved Ivory,' another F_1 hybrid, has creamy white flowers. Fruit Bowl is a mixture of all zinnia colors in very large cactus-type flowers. 'Blaze' (All-America) has red flowers fading to scarlet-orange. The Burpeeana strain is compact, growing about 18 to 24 inches tall with 5 to 6-inch flowers in mixed and single shades.

Dahlia Flowered and California Giant zinnias are very similar to one another and grow 2 to 3 feet tall with large, flat-petalled flowers unlike the spiky flowers of the Cactus types. 'Envy,' a Dahlia Flowered type has unique 3 to 4-inch double flowers, chartreuse in color.

Another large-flowered zinnia is State Fair, a tetraploid strain growing 30 to 36 inches with 5 to 6-inch double flowers in the full range of zinnia colors. Plants are highly resistant to mildew.

Of medium flower size are Peppermint Stick and Whirligig, attractive striped and bicolor types of the cut-and-come-again variety (*Z. elegans* 'Pumila').

Among the smaller zinnias, varieties in the Peter Pan strain (All-America) grow only 10 to 12 inches tall, have fully double 3-inch blooms, and are outstanding massed in borders or used as edgings.

Lilliput or Pompon types (such as the Button series) are bushy and rounded growing to 2 feet tall with 2-inch blooms in single and mixed colors.

An extra-dwarf zinnia is 'Thumbelina,' just 6 inches tall and covered with 1½-inch double and semidouble flowers in lavender, orange, pink, scarlet, white, and yellow.

TORENIA

VIRGINIAN STOCK

VERBENA

ZINNIA 'THUMBELINA'

Index

Photographers

William Aplin: 12 (bottom), 23 (top right); **George J. Ball, Inc.:** 41 (center left); **Glenn Christiansen:** 23 (bottom left and right); **Ferry-Morse Seed Company:** 31 (top left); **Ells Marugg:** 8 (all), 11, 12 (top left and right), 18 (all), 20 (top and bottom left), 21 (top, center, bottom left), 23 (top left), 26 (all), 28 (all), 29 (all), 31 (bottom left, top and bottom right), 33 (all), 35 (all), 38 (all), 40 (all), 41 (top and bottom left, center right), 43 (all), 46 (all), 48 (all), 50 (all), 52 (all), 53 (all), 55 (all), 58 (all), 60 (all), 61 (all); **Don Normark:** 14 (all); **Norman A. Plate:** 15, 20 (top and bottom right), 21 (top right); **Darrow Watt:** 10 (all).